GEM TRAILS

▄▄▄ OF ▄▄▄

SOUTHERN CALIFORNIA

By *James R. Mitchell*

Gem Guides Book Co.

315 Cloverleaf Drive, Suite F
Baldwin Park, CA 91706

Library of Congress Control Number: 2002116086
ISBN 1-889786-25-X

Maps: Janet Francisco and Jean Hammond
Cover Art: Scott Roberts

NOTE:
  Due to the possibility of personal error, typographical error, misinterpretation of information, and the many changes due to man or nature, *Gem Trails of Southern California*, its publisher, and all other persons directly or indirectly associated with this publication, assume no responsibility for accidents, injury, or any losses by individuals or groups using this publication.
  In rough terrain and hazardous areas, all persons are advised to be aware of possible changes due to man or nature that occur along the gem trails.

PUBLISHED BY:
Gem Guides Book Co.
315 Cloverleaf Drive, Suite F
Baldwin Park, CA 91706
www.gemguidesbooks.com
gembooks@aol.com

TABLE OF CONTENTS

Table of Contents

KEY TO SITE LOCATOR MAP

Site No.

REGION I
(1) Jacumba Minerals
(2) Anza-Borrego
(3) Plaster City
(4) Yuha Basin
(5) Rainbow Rock
(6) Winterhaven Geodes
(7) Gold Basin
(8) Cargo Muchacho Mountains
(9) Coon Hollow
(10) Hauser Beds
(11) Black Hills Minerals
(12) Pebble Terrace
(13) Opal Hill Mine
(14) Little Chuckwalla Mountains
(15) Chuckwalla Well
(16) Chuckwalla Spring
(17) Blythe
(18) Red Cloud Jasper
(19) Orocopa Mountains Fluorite

REGION II
(20) Vidal Junction
(21) Big Rover
(22) Turtle Mountains
(23) Lake Havasu
(24) Danby
(25) Cadiz
(26) Chambless
(27) Orange Blossom Copper
(28) Kelbaker Road
(29) Ludlow Obsidian
(30) Cady Mountains
(31) Bristol Mountains Onyx
(32) Broadwell Dry Lake
(33) Lavic Jasper
(34) Hector Hills
(35) Jasper Hill
(36) Newberry Nodules and Agate
(37) Ord Mountain
(38) Stoddard Well

Site No.

REGION III
(39) San Gabriel Mountains Actinolite
(40) Newhall Fossils
(41) Castle Butte
(42) North Edwards Onyx
(43) Kramer Hills
(44) Opal Mountain
(45) Coyote Dry Lake
(46) Calico Mountains
(47) Yermo
(48) Afton Canyon
(49) Alvord Mountains
(50) Field Road
(51) Toltec Mine
(52) Zabriskie Station Opal
(53) Tecopa Minerals
(54) Kingston Mountain
(55) El Paso Mountains
(56) Steam Well
(57) Bedrock Spring
(58) Rainbow Ridge
(59) Sheep Springs
(60) Trona Onyx
(61) Ballarat
(62) Olancha Fossils
(63) Cerro Gordo Fossils
(64) Lone Pine Ammonites

REGION IV
(65) Topanga Fossils
(66) Acton
(67) Rincon Fossils
(68) Santa Barbara Fossils
(69) Cinco Crystals
(70) Brown Butte
(71) Rosamond Collectibles
(72) Lake Cachuma
(73) Los Olivos
(74) Jalama Beach
(75) San Luis Obispo
(76) Cambria Moonstone
(77) Devils Den Fossils
(78) Kettleman Hills
(79) Ant Hill Shark's Teeth
(80) Coalinga
(81) Clear Creek
(82) Junnila Claims

SOUTHERN CALIFORNIA SITE LOCATOR MAP

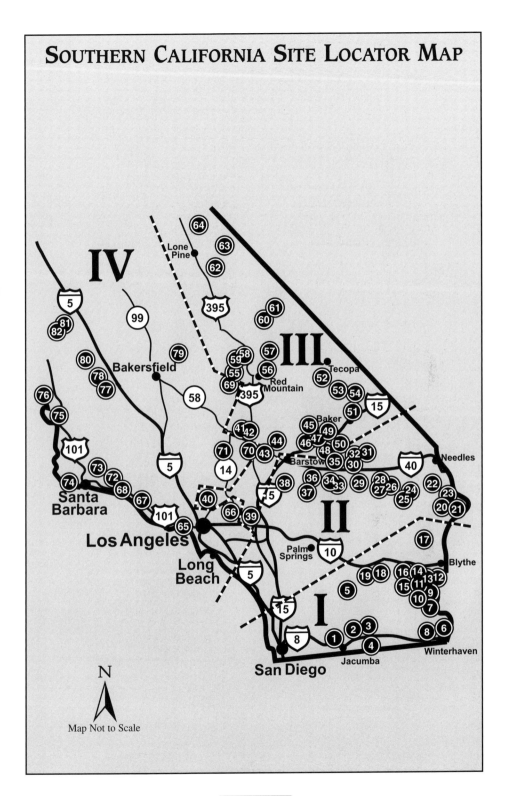

IV

64
Lone Pine
63
62

5
81
82

99

395
61
60

80
Bakersfield
79
78
77
76
75

III.

58
59
55
69

57
56
Red Mountain
395

Tecopa
52
53 54
51
15

58

101
73
72
68
67
Santa Barbara

5
14

71 70 43
41 42
44

45
46 47 49
48 50
Barstow 35
30
32 31

Baker

40

Needles

74
101
65

40
66 39

38
36 34
37 33
29
28
27 26
25
24

22
23
20 21

II

Los Angeles

Long Beach

5

Palm Springs
10

5

17

19 18
5

16 14
15 11 13 12
10 9
7

Blythe

I

15

8
1 2 3
4

8 6

San Diego
Jacumba
Winterhaven

N

Map Not to Scale

Map Legend

══════⬡80══════	Interstate Highway
──────⬡93──────	U.S. Highway
──────(225)──────	State Highway
──────[81]──────	County Road
──────────────	Local Road
‑ ‑ ‑ ‑ ‑ ‑ ‑ ‑	Gravel Graded Road
══════════════	Graded Dirt Road
▪▪▪▪▪▪▪▪▪▪▪▪▪▪	Unimproved Dirt Road
‑‑‑‑‑‑‑‑‑‑‑‑‑‑	Trail
▬ ▬ ▬ ▬ ▬ ▬ ▬	Border, Boundary, State Line
⟨X⟩	Collecting Spot
⬭	Lake, River, Reservoir, Aqueduct, Creek, Wash
🌢	Well
≣	Cattle Guard
⊠	Gate
Λ	Campground
♠♠	Store, Station
⚒	Mine
⋈	Recreation/Picnic Area
♠	School
⚑	Milepost
▫	Ruin
─□─	Exit
⌸ ⬡	Sign or Stop Sign
═══	Road Map Break

INTRODUCTION

NEW DESERT REGULATIONS

It is important to note that there have been numerous regulatory changes governing travel and access to the deserts and mountains of southern California since *Gem Trails of Southern California* was last published. State and Federal Park boundaries have been greatly expanded, including Joshua Tree National Park and Death Valley National Park. To further restrict desert access to all but the most physically fit, the 1.4 million acre Mojave National Preserve was established as were another sixty-nine wilderness areas encompassing an additional 3.6 million acres. Each has different governing regulations and it is imperative that you confirm what is allowed and what is not allowed before venturing in. For the most part, none permit any type of motorized transportation or equipment within their boundaries, but all do allow foot travel. Absolutely no rock or mineral collecting is permitted within any State or Federal Park as well as the Mojave National Preserve. Casual collecting is still authorized in the sixty-nine BLM Wilderness Areas, but all access must be on foot. The BLM notes that casual use activities include small scale recreational rockhounding that utilizes non-mechanical hand tools such as small picks and shovels, and what is gathered must be for non-commercial purposes. Absolutely no mechanized or heavy digging is permitted and no visible scars on the landscape may be left behind. All of these restricted regions are well signed with boundary markers but, as is the case all too often, some of them may have been removed or destroyed by vandals. That, obviously, does not mean you can "claim ignorance" and drive in. Be aware of the restricted regions and honor their regulations and restrictions. If a particular site lies in or close to any wilderness area, the author has attempted to note such information and provide good suggested parking spots, but it is the reader's responsibility to make the final determination as to exactly where to park, what to collect and how to do it.

Gathering wood for campfires within the wilderness areas, when permitted, is limited to dead and down materials. Live vegetation cannot be cut. If you choose to hike to a collecting spot situated inside a wilderness area, be certain to take sufficient water, take a cell phone, don't go in the sweltering summer months, wear proper clothing and footwear, do not lose track of where you are, and, most importantly, do not attempt doing something you are not physically capable of doing. Extended hikes in the desert, especially when carrying supplies, can be life threatening.

It is also important to note that any off-road driving is strictly prohibited in most parts of the desert, even in regions outside the protected areas. If you have further questions about any aspect of these new laws governing wilderness areas or the desert in general, be sure to inquire at a local BLM Office as listed in the Government Agencies list in the back of this book, or contact the BLM California Desert District, 6221 Box Springs Boulevard, Riverside, CA 92507-0714; (909) 697-5200.

HOW TO USE THIS GUIDEBOOK

This guide provides detailed travel descriptions to eighty-two collecting sites within Southern California. Each is accompanied by a detailed map and, in many cases, a photograph. Mileage is as accurate as possible, but odometers on all vehicles do vary and distances have been rounded to the nearest tenth of a mile. The sites are located in landscapes as full of variety as the minerals themselves. The terrain includes pine covered mountains, barren deserts, beautiful beaches and just about everything in between.

Be advised that the maps are intentionally NOT DRAWN TO SCALE. The purpose is to provide a single illustration showing the general setting, with more detailed travel instructions near the site itself.

Some of the locations discussed in the book are difficult to get to, and pertinent warning and advice is provided in the accompanying text. Even in cases where there are no warnings, however, it is essential you remember that road conditions do change. Severe weather can make good roads very rough, and very rough roads totally impassable, even with four-wheel drive. You must decide for yourself what your particular vehicle is capable of. Do not go where your car was not designed to go!

Some of the spots mentioned are situated on the dumps of old and abandoned mines. Do not, under any circumstances, enter the shafts, and always be cautious when exploring the surrounding regions. There are often hidden tunnels, rotten ground, pits, rusty nails, broken glass and discarded chemicals, all of which can create potential hazards.

A few of the sites are on private property and access is not guaranteed, or, possibly, a fee may be charged to collect there. Fee information and land status is discussed in the text, as it was at time of publication, but DO NOT ASSUME THAT THIS GUIDE GIVES PERMISSION TO COLLECT! Land status changes frequently. Many sites are being closed to the public, due to rising insurance costs and a surge in frivolous lawsuits. If you have a suspicion that a particular spot is no longer open, be sure to check before trespassing. If nothing can be determined locally, land ownership information is always available at the County Recorder's office.

SOME REMINDERS

Collectors are reminded of government regulations about gathering petrified wood. Rockhounds can obtain no more than 25 pounds of petrified wood per day, plus one piece, and no more than 250 pounds per year. To acquire a specimen weighing more than 250 pounds, a permit must be procured from the District Manager of the Bureau of Land Management. Groups cannot pool their allocations together, and wood from public lands cannot be bartered or sold to commercial dealers, and may only be obtained with hand tools.

There are also some recent restrictions related to the gathering of fossils, especially within National Forests, and it is advisable that you try to keep up to date with those ever changing laws and regulations. Primarily, the collection of vertebrate fossils is illegal on public lands without a paleontological permit. Permits to paleontologists are available at BLM offices. It also should be noted that prehistoric artifacts made of agate, chalcedony, jasper, obsidian, chert and other similar stones, that have historically been used by Native Americans in the building of weapons or tools, cannot be collected on public lands without an archaeological permit (also obtainable at a BLM Office).

CONCLUSION

Generally, the weather in Southern California is pleasant during the winter months, especially in the deserts, but rain is always a possibility. Summers, however, can get very hot, with temperatures often soaring well above 100° F, especially in the deserts. For that reason, it is strongly suggested that you do not do any desert rockhounding during that time of year. The spring and fall tend to be the best times to fully explore Southern California.

When venturing into some of the more remote areas, it is a good idea to take extra drinking water, foul weather clothing, a cell phone, and even some food, just in case you get delayed or stuck. If you take the time to properly plan your trip and make sure your vehicle is in good working order, the gem fields listed on the following pages will provide you and your family with countless hours of collecting pleasure, fine mineral specimens, and many memorable experiences.

James R. Mitchell

Road to Acton Collecting Area Site A

Various BLM Signs to Be Aware of in the Field.

ROCKHOUND RULES

The following are a few basic rules that should always be followed no matter what state or country you are collecting in.

(1) Tell someone where you are going and what time you expect to return.

(2) Do not collect alone—have at least one companion with you.

(3) Wear appropriate clothing: long pants; work boots, preferably with steel toes; a hard hat if working around vertical rock faces; heavy work gloves; and protective eye wear if you are going to be hammering.

(4) Research the area you are going to—what kind of vehicle is needed to get there; what is to be found; are there old mine shafts you should be aware of or other dangers; and what kind of equipment will you need.

(5) Always ask permission to enter a property if possible.

(6) Leave all gates in the position that you found them.

(7) Do not disturb livestock.

(8) Never, ever litter. If possible, leave the place cleaner than it was when you arrived.

(9) Do not "hog" the site or make it difficult for the next person to collect.

(10) Do not leave children or pets unattended. They can get into serious trouble.

(11) Never leave fires unattended, and do not light them in dry, hazardous conditions.

(12) Bring a first aid kit with you and know how to use it in case someone is in need of medical attention.

(13) Never enter abandoned mines without proper training, equipment and permission—and never alone.

Although there are hundreds of places to collect throughout California, there are places you cannot. Collecting is never allowed in national monuments or federal and state parks. Non-commercial hobby collecting is allowed in areas under the management of the U.S. Forest Service and the Bureau of Land Management. See the Introduction for specific rules and regulations.

Enjoy your collecting and the wonderful hobby that we all share. Be safe, obey the laws. Always be considerate and we will have a hobby for many years to come. Remember, all it takes is one thoughtless person to close down a collecting locality.

HINTS FOR COLLECTING MINERALS

Following are some suggestions for collecting minerals:

(1) Necessary items are a prospector's pick, safety goggles, gloves, wrapping materials, hand lens, notebook, pen and hand rake. Your equipment should also include items from the following categories and possibly some of these options.

- *Shovels:* collapsible shovel, spade, miner's shovel
- *Large Picks:* miner's pick, 16-inch ore pick
- *Striking Tools:* crack hammer, chisel point pick, maul
- *Chisels:* cold chisel, wedge, gad, screwdriver
- *Options:* hydraulic jack, augers, hand drill, bent wire

(2) When working in a mine dump look for any mineral which is different from the rest of the pile in color, translucency, shape, luster or texture.

(3) Look for specimens which are combinations of several minerals.

(4) Work with someone. When there is heavy digging or rock moving, alternate jobs.

(5) Look for cavities in the rock walls.

(6) Split large rocks which are composed of several minerals.

(7) Look for a contact zone, an area where two different types of rock meet.

(8) Micromounts are found in small seams, vugs, old natural fractures, between mica and feldspar plates and in loose coarse material. Examine all specimens with suspected micromount qualities with a 10-power hand lens.

(9) If you find a good specimen, try to trace where it came from.

(10) If you are in a mine or quarry, identify the principal rocks, know what minerals may be found with them, and seek out any layer which shows the characteristics you are looking for. Prospect several areas quickly before selecting a place to dig.

(11) A water bottle with sprayer is handy on old mine dumps.

(12) Investigate the ground around old dumps and old mines.

Excerpted from Midwest Gem, Fossil, and Mineral Trails: Prairie States, *by June Culp Zeitner.*

HINTS FOR COLLECTING GEM MATERIALS

Following are some suggestions for collecting gem materials:

(1) Walk back and forth looking at the rocks with the sun in front of you and then behind you. Agates and chalcedony are translucent with the light shining through them. Patterns show off better with the sun behind you.

(2) Look for gemstones after rains, if possible. Moisture makes the patterns and color stand out.

(3) Learn to check rocks in the field. A small chip can be knocked off from the edge with a prospector's pick. Holding the rock firm with one hand and strike it quickly at the edge with a hard blow. Let your wrist give with the blow.

(4) If a rock is already broken, a conchoidal fracture is often a sign it is polishable.

(5) Look in streams and along lakes, and also on the grassy hillsides and dirt banks along the lakes and streams.

(6) If a rock is of good color but badly fractured, remember your tumbler.

(7) Agates may have oxidized coatings. They may also have thumbprint depressions or pockmarks.

(8) Make a record on the spot of any find you make which is strange or unusual in any way.

(9) A spray bottle of water will help determine the characteristics of individual gem materials.

Excerpted from Midwest Gem, Fossil, and Mineral Trails: Prairie States, *by June Culp Zeitner.*

JACUMBA MINERALS

This location gets mixed reviews, but provides a great place to stop and stretch your legs when traveling on Interstate Highway 8. The site has provided patient collectors fine specimens of rainbow quartz, shimmering moonstone and even some small but well formed garnet crystals.

To get to there, travel along Interstate Highway 8 about 70 miles east from San Diego or 50 miles west from El Centro to the In-Ko-Pah Park Exit and go north to where the access road ends. At that point, turn left (west) and proceed about 0.2 miles to pavement's end. From there, you can either hike straight ahead to Site A on what was once the main road, or drive along the rough tracks leading off to the right to Site B. Both roads proceed about 0.2 miles to different parts of collecting area, and it might prove fruitful to try each of them. If you choose to drive the old ruts leading to the old mine at Site B, be certain that your vehicle is capable, since this is not a route for passenger cars. Otherwise, simply hike the short distance.

At time of publication, both of these mines were abandoned, but, as is always the case, be certain that is still the situation when you visit. Site A gives the greatest likelihood of procuring some of the moonstone variety of feldspar. The primary deposit is on the upper hillside, but suitable pieces can be found amongst the rubble lower down. The garnet and rainbow quartz are more prevalent at and around the old mine at Site B. As was the case at Site A, look in the mining areas as well as surrounding hills. The rainbow quartz

is best found by splitting suspect pieces and carefully examining the fresh surface for signs of color. The finest specimens, when properly cut and polished, will display fine star-like cat's-eye, which are very prized by lapidary artists. Garnet crystals are also found here, generally embedded within the tough host rock. Chunks containing a lot of the little garnets are great for display in a mineral collection.

The Road Leading From the Pavement to the Site

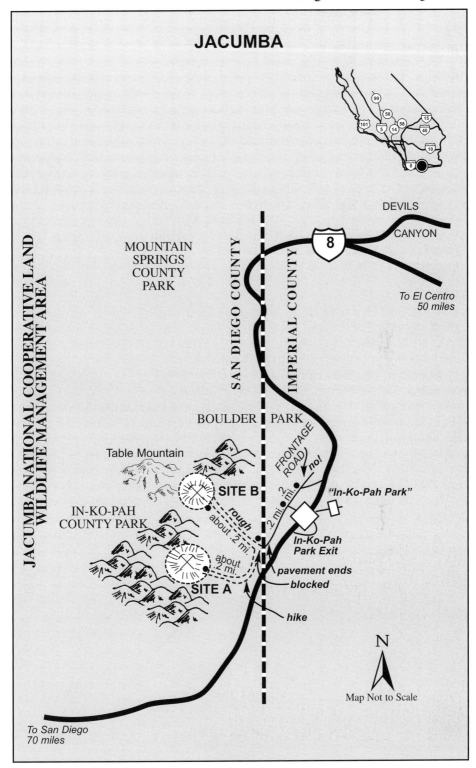

JACUMBA

JACUMBA NATIONAL COOPERATIVE LAND
WILDLIFE MANAGEMENT AREA

MOUNTAIN
SPRINGS
COUNTY
PARK

SAN DIEGO COUNTY

IMPERIAL COUNTY

DEVILS

CANYON

8

To El Centro
50 miles

BOULDER PARK

Table Mountain

FRONTAGE
ROAD

no!

SITE B

"In-Ko-Pah Park"

IN-KO-PAH
COUNTY PARK

.2 mi.

.2 mi.

rough
about .2 mi.

about
.2 mi.

In-Ko-Pah
Park Exit

pavement ends

blocked

SITE A

hike

N

Map Not to Scale

To San Diego
70 miles

ANZA-BORREGO

The three sites illustrated on the accompanying map offer a good opportunity to gather fine samples of fossilized shells, agate, jasper and selenite. Site A is situated just before entering the newly designated Coyote Mountains Wilderness Area and centers around a series of sand hills. Throughout those hills can be found a lot of frequently clear selenite slabs "growing" out of the soft soil. They are bright white and, therefore easily spotted—contrasting sharply with the brown sand. It takes very little work to remove a number of specimens. Simply dig into the soft soil with a hand rake or trowel wherever you happen to see the slabs. In addition to mineral collecting, the view from the hills affords a nice desert panorama.

To get to Site B, Fossil Canyon, continue through the wash to the markers designating the wilderness boundary. Be very careful not to get stuck in the loose sand. If your vehicle is not capable of traveling on such terrain, it is suggested that you hike rather than drive. From the wilderness boundary, you must hike into Fossil Canyon which is filled with fossil shells and onyx, with the latter generally being white, light pink and green. Simply examine the rocks and boulders lying in the washes and lowlands. It should also be noted that many of the shells and fossil fish skeletons fluoresce under a blacklight. If you are careful when scrambling around in the dark, spending the night here with a blacklight can prove to be very fruitful, as well as lots of fun.

Painted Gorge, Site C, offers more fossils, as well as some scattered agate and jasper. This is regarded as one of the most scenic regions of the Colorado Desert and a side trip into the colorful gorge is worth the time, even if you don't do any collecting. The agate and jasper are sparsely scattered through-out the region, primarily to the south, while the blocky fossil-bearing rock can easily be seen crumbling from the hills and cliffs in the area shown.

Due to the locality's sandy hills, this spot has also become very popular with off-road vehicle drivers. For that reason, be very cautious. Some of the off-roaders travel at unreasonably high speeds, and it isn't uncommon to encounter very young drivers.

Site C Collecting Area

ANZA-BORREGO

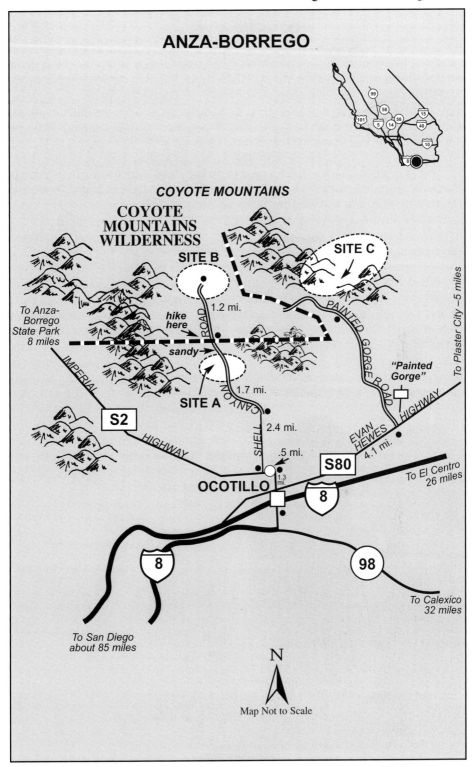

COYOTE MOUNTAINS

**COYOTE
MOUNTAINS
WILDERNESS**

SITE B

SITE C

1.2 mi.

To Anza-
Borrego
State Park
8 miles

hike
here

sandy→

To Plaster City –5 miles

PAINTED GORGE ROAD

"Painted
Gorge"

1.7 mi.

SITE A

IMPERIAL

S2

2.4 mi.

SHELL CANYON ROAD

HIGHWAY

EVAN
HEWES

HIGHWAY

.5 mi.

4.1 mi.

1.3 mi.

S80

To El Centro
26 miles

OCOTILLO

8

8

98

To Calexico
32 miles

To San Diego
about 85 miles

N

Map Not to Scale

PLASTER CITY

Both of these sites are extensive, and material can be found for quite a distance in all directions from the specific locations shown on the accompanying map. Throughout the desert region northwest of Plaster City collectors can find very nice and sometimes sizable pieces of petrified wood, as well as occasional chunks of agate, jasper and selenite. Be advised that virtually all roads traverse regions of very loose sand. When driving through here, you may reach a point where it might be advisable to park and walk, rather than risk getting stuck.

Site A is noted for its well formed petrified wood. Most is small, but rains frequently expose large limb sections. The wood is randomly scattered throughout the hills and washes, and patient searching is required. Just park somewhere in the general area and start hiking. Once you find the first piece of petrified wood, and see exactly what it looks like, subsequent specimens seem easier to find. Much is a very nice light brown/tan color, sometimes filled with colorful orange stringers.

Site B not only boasts additional wood, but is also a good place to gather fragile slabs of selenite. They are easily seen "growing" out of the sand cliffs in and around the region shown on the map. This spot is somewhat difficult to find, since there are so many tracks throughout the area. But, if you are patient, and head in the proper direction, you should have no major problem. Scant amounts of agate, jasper and chalcedony can also be picked up throughout the desert areas encompassed by both sites, so be on the lookout. As was the case at Site A, the best method for collecting here is to park at the hills and explore on foot as much of the nearby region as you have time and energy for.

It should be mentioned that this locality is frequently used by off-road vehicle enthusiasts, especially during the winter months.

Well formed Petrified Wood Found at Site A

PLASTER CITY

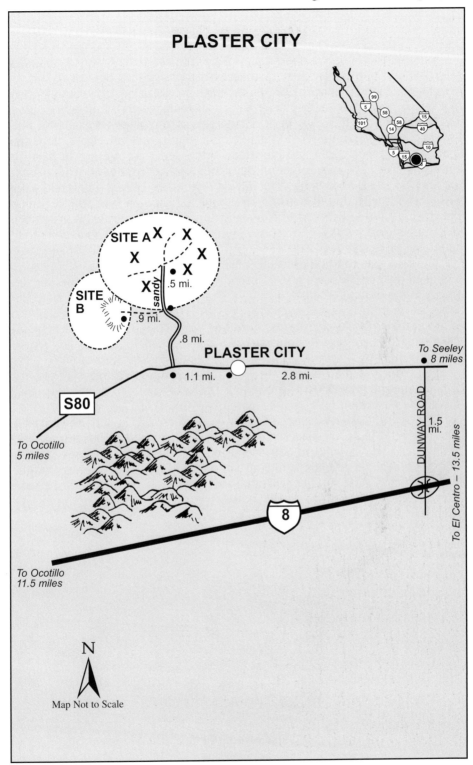

SITE A

X X
X X
X
.5 mi.
X

sandy

SITE B

.9 mi.

.8 mi.

PLASTER CITY

To Seeley
8 miles

1.1 mi.   2.8 mi.

S80

To Ocotillo
5 miles

DUNWAY ROAD

1.5 mi.

To El Centro – 13.5 miles

8

To Ocotillo
11.5 miles

N

Map Not to Scale

YUHA BASIN

These sites are only a short distance from Interstate Highway 8 and offer the rockhound an opportunity to collect a variety of materials. It should be mentioned, though, that the roads cut through areas of clay, making them impassable when wet, even if your vehicle is equipped with four-wheel drive.

To get to Site A, simply park off the ruts at the given mileage and hike toward the green and white hills to the south. As you walk, look for chalcedony, jasper, agate and obsidian. These gems are not overly plentiful since this spot is so easy to get to, but some pieces are quite colorful, usually making the effort worthwhile. The hills at Site A are covered with rocks filled with fossil shells. It takes some time and patience to find the very best specimens, but that extra effort is usually rewarded. You may want to do some pick and shovel work in order to uncover less weathered and potentially better pieces.

At Site B, one can find unusual, spherical concretions in areas surrounding the hill shown on the map. Just do some walking for quite a distance, keeping an eye to the ground. These unusual mineralogical oddities range in size from about an inch in diameter to some measuring over 1 foot across. They are found in many fascinating forms, including dumbbells or cones, but most are spherical. They are usually concentrically-layered, making it easy to "repair" damaged ones by chipping off an outer layer to thereby form a perfect, but smaller, replica of the original. As was the case at Site A, this site has also been thoroughly picked over throughout the years and decent specimens are few and far between.

Site C, only a short distance farther along the road, is part of what local collectors refer to as the Oyster Beds. There, virtually every hill is littered with fossil-filled rocks, similar to that at Site A. In addition, rockhounds can find occasional selenite crystals "growing" in the soft soil. They are very fragile, though, and should be handled and transported with utmost care. Better selenite and fossils can often be procured by cautiously using a small hand rake and/or trowel to unearth otherwise hidden but better protected specimens.

Unusual Spherical Concretions at Site B

YUHA BASIN

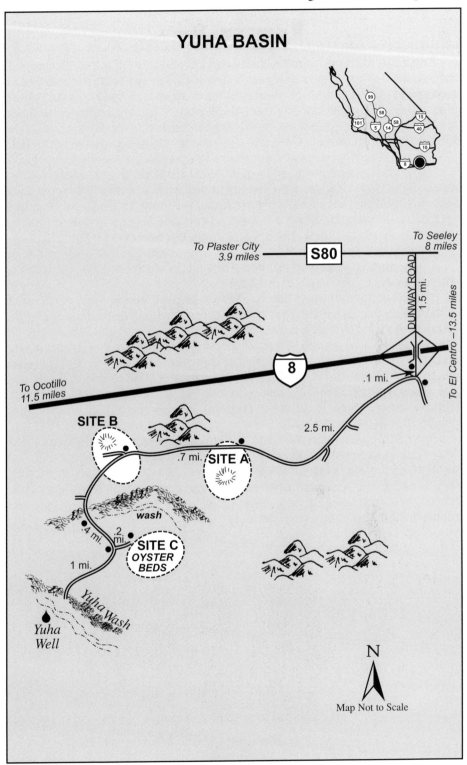

To Plaster City
3.9 miles

S80

To Seeley
8 miles

To Ocotillo
11.5 miles

8

DUNWAY ROAD

1.5 mi.

To El Centro – 13.5 miles

.1 mi.

2.5 mi.

SITE B

.7 mi.

SITE A

wash

.4 mi.

.2 mi.

SITE C
*OYSTER
BEDS*

1 mi.

Yuha Wash

*Yuha
Well*

N

Map Not to Scale

RAINBOW ROCK

Good specimens of colorful jasper and rhyolite can be found just west of the Salton Sea. This trip is only for those with a four-wheel drive vehicle or a willingness to hike through deep sand for about 1.5 miles. In fact, even four-wheel drive vehicles may have problems navigating amongst the large boulders littering the wash. Be further advised that this location is within the Torres Martinez Indian Reservation and information about any restrictions in place at the time of your visit can usually be obtained in Coolidge Springs.

To get to Rainbow Rock, the center of this difficult to access location, go south along State Highway 86 for 5.8 miles from where it intersects State Highway 195. At that point is a paved road on the west leading to Coolidge Springs. Take that road about 1.8 miles to Coolidge Springs and then, instead of continuing along the pavement back to the highway, follow the rutted Pole Line Road as it proceeds south. Drive approximately 1.9 more miles to Wonderstone Wash. Turn right, enter that large wash, and go 1.2 miles to where it skirts to the south of the hills.

This final drive through the wash is where most people have problems. It is slightly uphill, there are a lot of tight turns, and boulders are encountered all along the way. In fact, it is sometimes necessary to stop and roll large rocks clear in order to continue. That, of course, destroys your momentum and makes it difficult to get going again in the deep sand. If you reach a point where your vehicle can no longer safely continue, it is advisable that you stop and walk the remaining distance. Do not get stuck, since help is quite a distance away. There is an old abandoned bus on the left, at the stopping point, but it is difficult to spot.

Most of the hillside to the north of the wash, as shown on the map, offers jasper and nice rhyolite. Material can not only be found on the hill, but throughout the lowlands for quite a distance. The jasper occurs in browns, tans, white, cream and other earth tones. Some also contains showy moss patterns. Most will take a very nice polish and can be used to produce cabochons and other lapidary items.

RAINBOW ROCK

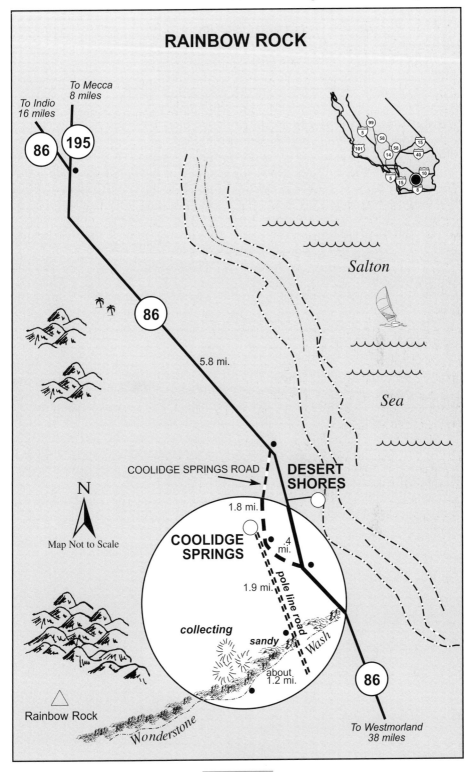

To Indio
16 miles

To Mecca
8 miles

86

195

86

5.8 mi.

Salton

Sea

COOLIDGE SPRINGS ROAD

DESERT
SHORES

1.8 mi.

N

Map Not to Scale

COOLIDGE
SPRINGS

.4
mi.

pole line road

1.9 mi.

collecting

sandy

Wash

about
1.2 mi.

Rainbow Rock

Wonderstone

86

To Westmorland
38 miles

WINTERHAVEN GEODES

Some interesting little nodules and geodes can be found just off the All American Canal, about 15 miles northeast of Winterhaven. Since this site is so close to Winterhaven, Interstate Highway 8 and Imperial Dam, it has been well worked during the past few decades, leaving material only for those willing to work for it. To get to the first of many potentially productive geode-bearing hills, which are actually mounds resulting from the dumping of soil dug from the canals when they were being constructed over sixty years ago, take Interstate Highway 8 to Winterhaven, just west of the Colorado River. From town, go east about 1 mile to Road S-24, heading toward Picacho Peak. Proceed another 3.5 miles to Ross Road and then turn right, staying on S-24 all the way to Coles Corner Store, which will be on the left, about 6.5 miles farther.

From there, continue another 1 mile and then go left 0.1 miles to the dirt road paralleling the All American Canal. Turn left alongside the canal, and continue another 2 miles to where a crossing bridge will be encountered. Transit the canal, go left, following the canal on the other side, another 0.3 miles. At that point, on the right, there are some dirt mounds which mark the center of the primary collecting site. Park on the little flat area to the east of the first mound, being careful not to get into any sand, unless you have four-wheel drive.

These hills, and the many other similar ones all along the canals, conceal geodes, nodules, agate and chalcedony. Very little work is required here. The soft soil is constantly being eroded away, thereby continually exposing fresh, spherical nodules, geodes and other collectibles. Climb around looking for the telltale orbs, agate, jasper and other minerals. If you feel like digging, it might be productive, but, generally, just roaming throughout the dirt mounds is fruitful and far less strenuous. As mentioned earlier, if you have the time, it might be worthwhile to inspect other of the mounds which are encountered all along the these canals. Just don't block the roadway when you park and do not get onto terrain your vehicle is not designed to go. The canal roads are well-graded, and should present no problem to rugged vehicles, unless wet.

WINTERHAVEN

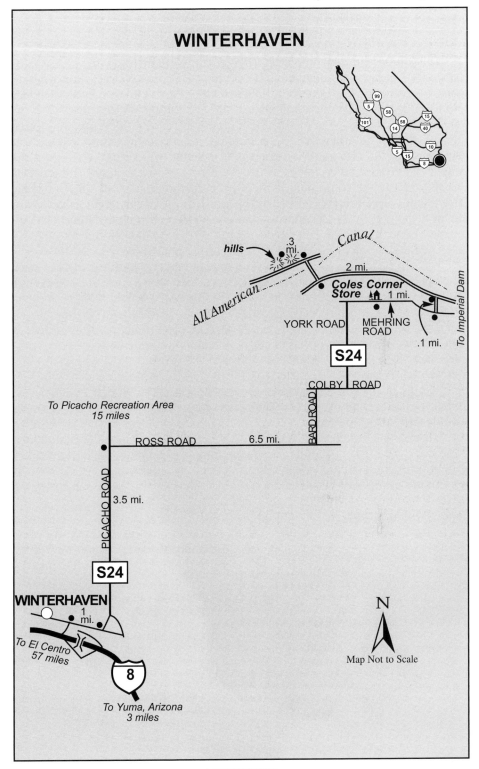

hills

.3. mi.

Canal

2 mi.

Coles Corner Store 1 mi.

All American

YORK ROAD

MEHRING ROAD

.1 mi.

To Imperial Dam

S24

COLBY ROAD

BARD ROAD

To Picacho Recreation Area
15 miles

ROSS ROAD   6.5 mi.

PICACHO ROAD

3.5 mi.

S24

WINTERHAVEN

1 mi.

To El Centro
57 miles

8

To Yuma, Arizona
3 miles

N

Map Not to Scale

GOLD BASIN

This part to the Colorado Desert is generally regarded as one of the most productive rockhounding regions in all of California. Collectors can unearth geodes ranging in size from very small to many inches across, as well as nice pieces of agate, chalcedony and jasper.

To get to Site A, which is the most productive of the three sites discussed here, follow State Highway 78 for 7.3 miles north from where it intersects Ogilby Road. At that point, on the right, is a hill with tracks leading up the side. Follow those steep tracks to the flat area on top and park. There isn't a lot of room on top, so no more than a few cars should plan on being up there at one time. If you don't feel your vehicle is capable of the climb, simply park down below and walk the short distance. Geodes and nodules are of primary interest here, and the digging areas are relatively easy to spot, due to the holes and mounds of soil left by previous collectors primarily on the north slopes.

You can continue excavating within existing pits or start one of your own. The soil is soft, making the work relatively easy, but a pick and shovel are essential. Many of the geodes are duds, but quite a few are filled with agate and/or beautiful crystals, with the prize being those filled with the spectacular red and orange agate that has made this area famous throughout the southwest.

One and two-tenths of a mile farther north on State Highway 78 are some more ruts that intersect from the east. Those lead to Site B, where you can gather chalcedony, pastel green agate and colorful jasper—most of which is found west of the hill near where you must park. More can be obtained just about anywhere in the area. The deep gorge east of the road contains additional cutting materials, as well as hematite pebbles. In the brown hills and steep wash south and west of the gorge, look for calcite crystals filling cracks and cavities of the native rock. Nothing is overly plentiful, and it takes patient searching to find worthwhile quantities of anything.

In and around the wash to the west of Midway Well, agate can be found, as can chalcedony, rhyolite, bright red jasper and occasional pieces of fire agate. This is labeled as Site C, and areas surrounding the dark brown desert varnished region, about 100 yards to the south, seem to offer the best concentrations. If you have time, be sure to explore other nearby washes, since most contain similar minerals in varying quantities and qualities.

Digging at Site A for Geodes and Nodules

GOLD BASIN

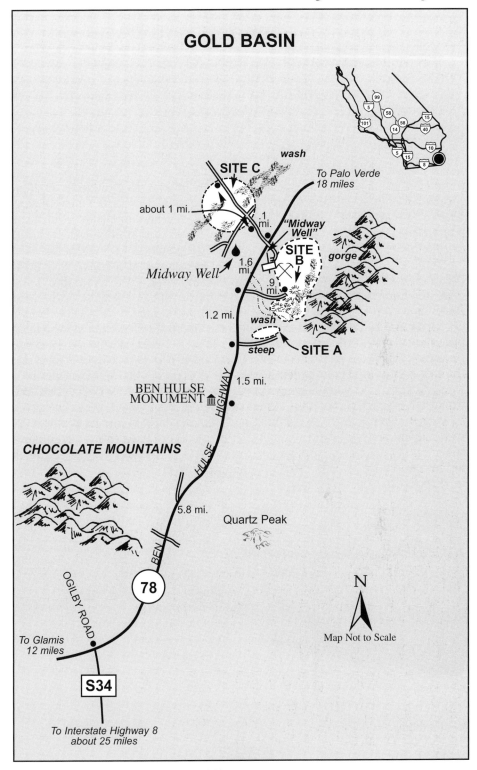

wash

SITE C

To Palo Verde
18 miles

about 1 mi.

.1 mi.

"Midway Well"

SITE B

gorge

Midway Well

1.6 mi.

.9 mi.

1.2 mi.

wash

steep

SITE A

1.5 mi.

BEN HULSE
MONUMENT

HIGHWAY

CHOCOLATE MOUNTAINS

HULSE

5.8 mi.

Quartz Peak

BEN

78

N

Map Not to Scale

OGILBY ROAD

To Glamis
12 miles

S34

To Interstate Highway 8
about 25 miles

CARGO MUCHACHO MOUNTAINS

Between the years 1925 and 1946, kyanite was removed from the Bluebird Mine, labeled as Site A on the accompanying map, and shipped to Los Angeles for use in kilns and furnaces. To get there, go north on Ogilby Road 4 miles to American Girl Mine Road, turn right and proceed 2 more miles to a fork. The right fork leads to a long abandoned quarry where rockhounds can find nice specimens of the sky-blue kyanite crystals embedded in host white quartz. The left fork goes to a more recent mining operation which may or may not be abandoned when you visit. If collecting is allowed there, material is easier to find due to its more recent exposure and less weathering. Look throughout the mine dumps and rubble as well as the surrounding boulders for the bladed, blue kyanite. Be also on the lookout for occasional limonite cubes which are scattered throughout the lower regions. BE REMINDED that the collecting status at either or both of these old mines is continually subject to change. It is your responsibility to determine if wherever you search is open. Otherwise restrict collecting to the washes and lowlands south and west of the mountain. If you have any doubts or concerns, it would be worthwhile to continue to the Gold Rock Ranch Store and get up to date information.

Site B is the famous Cargo Muchacho dumortierite location. Gem quality pieces of the beautiful dark blue/purple material are getting hard to find nowadays, but there are still some specimen grade chunks scattered throughout the hills and washes. In addition, there is occasional agate, jasper, petrified wood and petrified palm. To get there, go north on Ogilby Road for 4.8 miles from the Tumco Road intersection and turn right onto well-marked and graded Indian Pass Road. Drive 7.3 more miles to the center of Site B. Just park off the road and start hiking. The dumortierite is fairly easy to spot due to its blue color, but some looks almost black from a distance. This is a very well-known location and a lot of collecting has taken place over the years. It now takes a lot of patience to find specimens.

The Road Leading to the Collecting Area

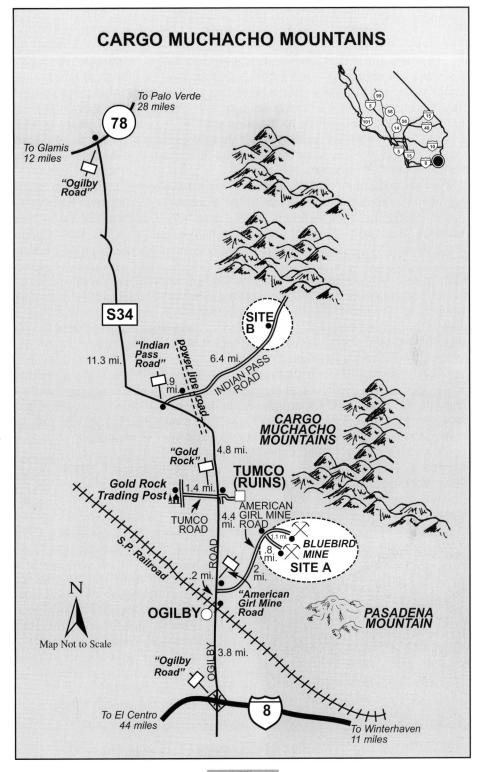

CARGO MUCHACHO MOUNTAINS

To Palo Verde
28 miles

78

To Glamis
12 miles

"Ogilby
Road"

S34

"Indian
Pass
Road"   power line road   6.4 mi.

11.3 mi.   .9
mi.   INDIAN PASS
ROAD

SITE
B

CARGO
MUCHACHO
MOUNTAINS

"Gold
Rock"   4.8 mi.

Gold Rock
Trading Post   1.4 mi.

TUMCO
ROAD   TUMCO
(RUINS)

AMERICAN
GIRL MINE
4.4 ROAD
mi.

1.1 mi.

BLUEBIRD
MINE

.8.
mi.   SITE A

S.P. Railroad

.2 mi.   2
mi.

"American
Girl Mine
Road   PASADENA
MOUNTAIN

OGILBY
ROAD

N

Map Not to Scale

"Ogilby
Road"   3.8 mi.

OGILBY

To El Centro
44 miles   8   To Winterhaven
11 miles

COON HOLLOW

This part of the Colorado Desert has been known by rockhounds for many years but still offers an amazing variety of minerals. Sites B, C, D, E and F are totally within the boundaries of the newly formed Palo Verde Wilderness Area, so the restrictions discussed in the Introduction apply at those locations. Most importantly, you cannot drive to the sites anymore, it is now necessary to hike. Use good judgment with regard to your physical condition, be sure to take some extra water, do not lose your bearings, and do not attempt the trek during the scorching summer months.

Access to all of the sites is from Milpitas Wash Road which intersects State Highway 78 about 11.5 miles south of Palo Verde, or from Interstate Highway 10 in the north at the Wiley Well Exit, about 13 miles west of Blythe. Mileages from either direction are provided on the accompanying map and Wiley Well/Milpitas Wash Road is well-graded and most rugged vehicles should have no problem traveling through here if driven carefully. Site A offers specimens of black psilomelane, some of which displays nice lumpy botryoidal occurrences, which make great specimens for mineral collections. The non-botryoidal material, which is much more prevalent, is still worth collecting, since, when cut and polished, it often shows little bands and circular patterns. Search the regions below the old mine as well as amongst the mine workings themselves, as long as the mine is still abandoned when you visit.

Sites B and C both offer collectors nice chunks of black seam agate and other more colorful varieties of that prized cutting material. Look in the cliffs to the north of the road for seams and in the regions below for material that has been weathered loose. To get to these sites a long hike is required and the material is not overly plentiful, so keep that in mind before making the trek.

More agate can be found at Sites D, E and F. At Site D, just as you rise from the wash, continuing about 0.5 miles farther, good material can be found throughout the obvious green soil, primarily to the north. Site E is accessed at the road's end, about 0.7 miles from the wash. Just park and follow the trail up the hill to the obvious excavations along the lower terrain. Agate seams will be spotted in the native rock, but most tend to be quite thin. The best hunting is in the washes and gullies, where good-sized chunks of jasp-agate can frequently be gathered,

some in bright hues of red and green. In addition, quartz crystals can be removed from cavities in the native rock, and chalcedony is scattered randomly, in a wide range of beautiful, pastel colors. There are geodes, nodules and banded agate at Site F.

Site G is yet another abandoned manganese mine where collectors can gather more of the nice black psilomelane in the same way as was done at Site A.

The Psilomelane Mine, Site A

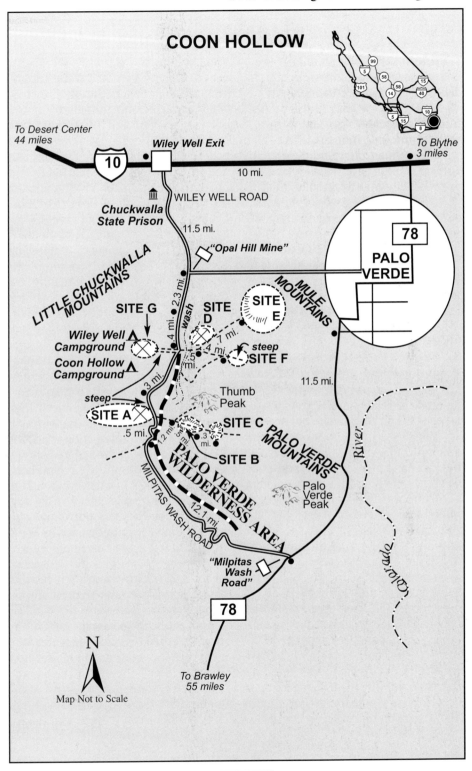

COON HOLLOW

To Desert Center
44 miles

10

Wiley Well Exit

To Blythe
3 miles

10 mi.

WILEY WELL ROAD

Chuckwalla
State Prison

11.5 mi.

"Opal Hill Mine"

78

**PALO
VERDE**

LITTLE CHUCKWALLA
MOUNTAINS

MULE
MOUNTAINS

2.3 mi.

wash

**SITE
D**

**SITE
E**

SITE G

.4 mi.

Wiley Well
Campground

.7 mi.

.4 mi.

steep

SITE F

Coon Hollow
Campground

.5
mi.

11.5 mi.

steep

3 mi.

Thumb
Peak

SITE A

.5 mi.

1.2 mi.

.6 mi.

.3
mi.

SITE C

SITE B

PALO VERDE
MOUNTAINS

River

PALO
VERDE
WILDERNESS
AREA

Palo
Verde
Peak

MILPITAS WASH ROAD

12.1 mi.

Colorado

"Milpitas
Wash
Road"

78

N

To Brawley
55 miles

Map Not to Scale

HAUSER BEDS

The Hauser Beds locality is arguably the southwest's best-known mineral collecting spot and, consequently, has recently been designated a Rockhound Educational and Recreational Area by the BLM. That means the BLM, instead of closing a good collecting area, has actually protected one. In addition, a new and much better maintained access road was opened and BLM signs help guide you along the way. The region boasts beautiful geodes, nodules and agate in numerous different digging areas which include, among others, the Hauser Beds, Corn Field, Potato Patch and Straw Beds. Remarkably, the supply has not substantially diminished over the years in spite of the amount of collecting that has been done. Don't be misled, though. It does take more effort and patience to find what, several years ago, could be simply picked up next to the road, but the material is still there.

The two major collecting areas are depicted on the accompanying map, but, as you will see, there are countless other diggings scattered throughout the region, any of which affords high potential for worthwhile collecting. Be advised that this part of the desert, even though open to collectors, is vehicle restricted. All vehicles must remain on designated roads and cross-country driving is prohibited. That necessitates hiking with pick and shovel to any spot off the main roads.

To get to the Hauser Beds region you have two choices. Take Milpitas Wash Road north from State Highway 78 about 10.3 miles to where the new access road intersects from the west or take Wiley Well Road south from where it intersects Interstate Highway 10 about 14 miles west of Blythe and then proceed 13.4 miles to the old access road, also intersecting from the west.

Whichever road you decide to take, follow the instructions on the accompanying map. Milpitas Wash/Wiley Well Road is well-graded and should not present a problem to most rugged vehicles. From the point where you head west the going is a little rougher, so use good judgment as to where your vehicle is capable of traveling. Four-wheel drive will probably not be needed. Site A is referred to as Potato Patch, best-known for its nice geodes, but equally as respected for the fine agate that can be found there. It is necessary to use a pick and shovel to dig for the geodes, but occasional agate specimens can be found on the surface.

The Hauser Beds, Site B, are reached by backtracking and then bearing southwest, as shown on the map. These diggings are extensive, and all you must do is look for the mounds left by previous rockhounds. DO NOT be tempted to do any tunneling while following seams of geodes at this or any other such location. A number of collectors have been buried when the very soft soil has collapsed over them. Always dig away overhangs, no matter how tempting it is to simply follow the geode-bearing strata. Beautiful orange and flame agate will also be encountered, as will very nice chalcedony. Many collectors feel that the agate is more valuable than the geodes and nodules, and, once you discover a piece of the best, you will probably understand why.

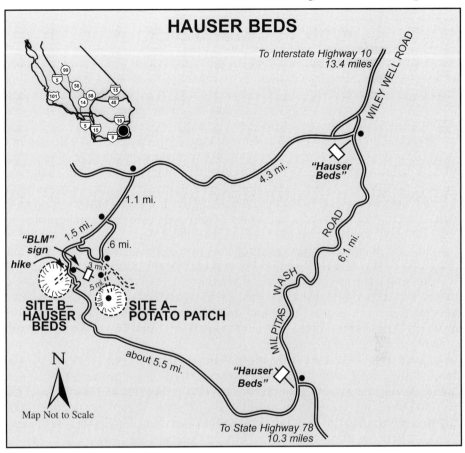

HAUSER BEDS

To Interstate Highway 10
13.4 miles

WILEY WELL ROAD

"Hauser Beds"

4.3 mi.

1.1 mi.

1.5 mi.

.6 mi.

"BLM" sign

hike

.3 mi.

.5 mi.

ROAD

6.1 mi.

SITE B–
HAUSER
BEDS

SITE A–
POTATO PATCH

WASH

MILPITAS

N

about 5.5 mi.

"Hauser Beds"

Map Not to Scale

To State Highway 78
10.3 miles

Parked at Site B

BLACK HILLS MINERALS

The Black Hills encompass much of the northwest portion of the renowned and highly-mineralized geode- and agate-bearing Wiley Well District. The four locations presented here offer collectors great opportunities to gather crystal- and agate-filled geodes, nodules, as well as chalcedony, agate, jasper and opalite.

To get to these sites you have two choices. Take Milpitas Wash Road north from State Highway 78 about 16.4 miles. You can also take the Wiley Well Road Exit from Interstate Highway 10 about 14 miles west of Blythe and then proceed south 13.4 miles as illustrated on the accompanying map. Milpitas Wash/Wiley Well Road is well-graded and should not present a problem to most rugged vehicles. From the point where you head west, the going is a little rougher, so use good judgment as to where your vehicle is capable of traveling. Four-wheel drive will probably not be needed with the possible exception of crossing the wash on the road leading to Site A.

From which ever direction you get to the access road, go west 5 miles to a major fork. Site A is reached by bearing left, crossing the wash and proceeding another 3.5 miles to the road's end and a great place to dig for geodes and agate. Digging with pick and shovel is the most efficient way to find acceptable quantities, but smaller chunks and chips can be found scattered all over the immediate area. Nothing above ground is very large, however, having been thoroughly picked over by previous rockhounds. Digging here in the soft ash-like soil is relatively easy and a good sturdy pick and shovel are the required tools. As is the case at any of the region's geode and nodule areas, DO NOT be tempted to do any tunneling. A number of collectors have been buried when the very soft soil has collapsed over them. Always dig away from overhangs, no matter how tempting it is to simply follow the geode-bearing strata.

To get to the other sites, return to the main road, bear west and proceed 3.2 miles. Site B is accessed by hiking across the wash which parallels the road and it boasts geodes, nodules and agate. Be careful when digging on the bank, making sure nothing falls on you from above. Go another 0.1 miles and either drive or hike to the base of the hill, (with the obvious mine workings up higher) that marking Site C. This location is renowned for its beautiful black agate and colorful opalite. The best is found by using hard rock tools to extract it from seams on the upper ridge, but a lot can be found throughout the lower hillsides, especially on the east. The final location, Site D, is another extensive agate, geode and chalcedony spot. Drive about 0.3 miles farther west to the road's end and then follow the trails leading from the parking area to the diggings.

BLACK HILLS

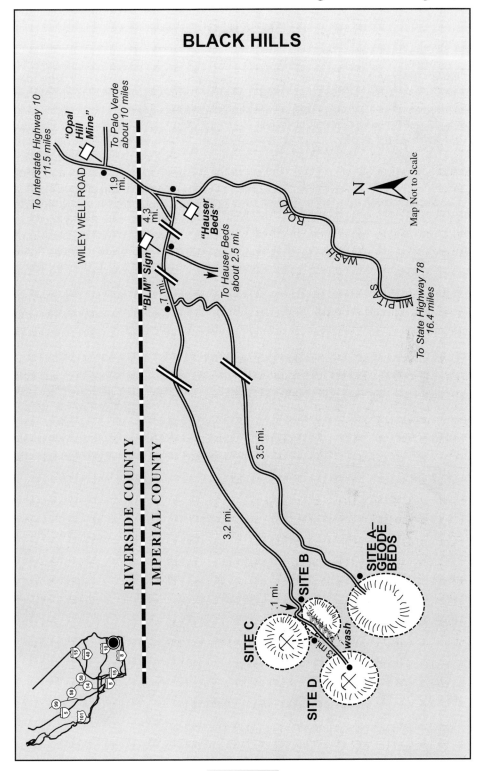

To Interstate Highway 10
11.5 miles

WILEY WELL ROAD

"Opal Hill Mine"

To Palo Verde
about 10 miles

1.9 mi.

4.3 mi.

"Hauser Beds"

"BLM" Sign

To Hauser Beds
about 2.5 mi.

.7 mi.

N

Map Not to Scale

WASH ROAD

MILPITAS WASH

To State Highway 78
16.4 miles

3.5 mi.

3.2 mi.

RIVERSIDE COUNTY

IMPERIAL COUNTY

.1 mi.

SITE B

SITE C

wash

SITE A—
GEODE BEDS

SITE D

PEBBLE TERRACE

Most of the desert pavement west of Palo Verde contains beautiful agate, jasper, chalcedony and occasional chunks of petrified wood. Much is concealed with a dark coating of desert varnish, making it difficult to spot. Collecting here requires a lot of patience and the willingness to split suspect stones to assist in proper identification. Considering the fine specimens that can be found, though, that extra effort is often rewarded with very colorful stones.

The agate and jasper is scattered throughout the flatlands, stretching west from Palo Verde all the way to the foothills, but the best concentrations seem to start about 5.8 miles from town, designated as Site A on the map. Occasionally, petrified wood, chalcedony roses and even spectacular fire agate can be found, especially as you approach the mountains. The wood tends to be light brown, but some are filled with bright orange stringers, making it especially desirable. Specimens with the dark brown and orange often take a beautiful polish and can be used to make exquisite jewelry or tumbled pieces. The roses are generally white, but some contain brown and orange swirls. Chalcedony with the brown and orange indicates the potential for internal "fire" and should be examined carefully. Sometimes wetting such stones will assist in determining if they do, in fact, contain a play of colors.

Keep in mind that this is a desert location and it gets extremely hot here in the summer months. Be sure to take something to drink, since working in this arid climate should make you very thirsty. Most of the roads are passable in rugged vehicles and four-wheel drive is not necessary, unless it is wet. Obviously, road conditions can change, so it is up to you to determine where your vehicle can go. There are also a few regions of soft sand, but, if you keep moving, they shouldn't cause a problem. If you decide to continue over the mountains to Coon Hollow, the road does get considerably rougher.

Desert Pavement at the Pebble Terrace Collecting Site

PEBBLE TERRACE

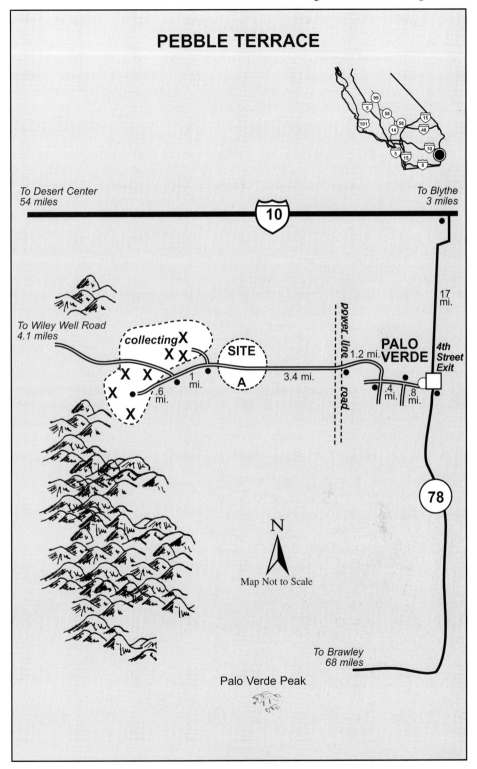

To Desert Center
54 miles

To Blythe
3 miles

10

To Wiley Well Road
4.1 miles

collecting X

X X

SITE

X X

X

X

1 mi.

.6 mi.

A

3.4 mi.

power line road

1.2 mi.

PALO VERDE

4th Street Exit

.4 mi.

.8 mi.

17 mi.

78

N

Map Not to Scale

To Brawley
68 miles

Palo Verde Peak

OPAL HILL MINE

This is a fee location situated just west of the Arizona/California border. This site is probably one of the best places to collect fire agate anywhere in the country, unless you own your own claim. As an added bonus, there are also a lot of nice chalcedony, agate, tiny quartz crystals, apatite, barite, calcite, clinoptilolite, fluorite, curved gypsum, and just across the road, some nice geodes.

To get to the Opal Hill Fire Agate Mine, go west from State Highway 78 on Fourth Street, at the southern edge of Palo Verde, as shown on the map. At the 1 mile mark, it will appear as if you are in someone's front yard, but the road goes around the house and heads through the sand hills toward the mountains. Follow the main road as it crosses Pebble Terrace, transits a couple of washes, and then heads into the mountains. Total distance from town is just under 9 miles, and the left-hand turn to the mine office can easily be seen at the given mileage. Your other choice is to take the Wiley Well Exit from Interstate Highway 10, about 13 miles west of Blythe and then proceed south 11.5 miles to where a sign designates the Opal Hill Mine Road 2 miles. Wiley Well Road is well-graded and should not present a problem to most rugged vehicles, but the trek over the little mountain to the mine is rough and rocky, making a high clearance rugged vehicle very desirable if not necessary.

There is a fee charged for each person per day, but there are weekly senior citizen and group rates available. The fee is a real bargain when you consider the value of what most people are able to find here. It isn't easy to remove the fiery gemstones from their place in the tough host rock. The mine owners, Nancy Hill and her husband Howard Fisher, are very helpful, and will make sure you get the most from your efforts. Be certain to take a good rock hammer, chisel, whisk broom, gloves, goggles and a long handled screw driver as a minimum tool supply, and be ready to do some tough work. In addition, take a lot to drink, since working in this arid climate can make you very thirsty, and the nearest supplies are 9 rough miles away in Palo Verde.

The geodes are found in a number of locations in and immediately surrounding the Opal Hill Mine, most notably, a new deposit recently discovered just across the canyon. Nancy or Howard will direct you to those locations when you are there. If you want to dig for the geodes, you will need a pick, shovel, hand trowel and other such equipment.

Camping is available at the mine, and there are even two campers and a little trailer that can be rented. They are open from November 1st until May 1st, and additional information can be obtained by writing to Nancy Hill, The Opal Hill Mine, P.O. Box 497, Palo Verde, CA 92266 or call (760) 854-3093.

OPAL HILL MINE

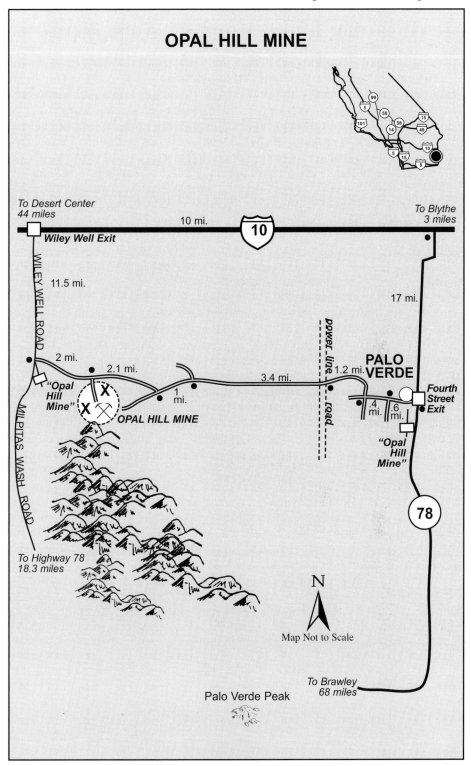

To Desert Center
44 miles

10 mi.

10

To Blythe
3 miles

Wiley Well Exit

WILEY WELL ROAD

11.5 mi.

17 mi.

2 mi.

2.1 mi.

power line road

1.2 mi.

PALO VERDE

Fourth Street Exit

"Opal Hill Mine"

X X

1 mi.

3.4 mi.

.4 mi.

.6 mi.

OPAL HILL MINE

"Opal Hill Mine"

MILPITAS WASH ROAD

78

To Highway 78
18.3 miles

N

Map Not to Scale

To Brawley
68 miles

Palo Verde Peak

LITTLE CHUCKWALLA MOUNTAINS

Neither of the two sites discussed here are within the boundaries of the newly formed Chuckwalla Mountains Wilderness Area, but Site A is very close. Be sure to read the Introduction in regard to limitations and restrictions if you choose to explore any of the lands within the wilderness area boundary. The sites boast a huge variety of collectibles, most notably agate, jasper, chalcedony, nodules, geodes, petrified wood and bark, perlite and even some tiny garnet crystals. Material can be found just about anywhere from the road to Site A, continuing west at least another 15 miles on either side of the Bradshaw Trail. For the most part, the concentrations are random, making collecting somewhat frustrating. The two sites discussed here have proven to be particularly reliable.

The first, labeled Site A on the accompanying map, offers an unusual agatized pine bark, as well as some fascinating geodes filled with bubbly chalcedony, scarce specimens of petrified wood, and a green hued variety of perlite. To get there, take the Bradshaw Trail Road for 10 miles west from where it intersects Wiley Well Road just south of the Wiley Well Campground. At that point, there is a rough little road leading to some mines in the hills to the north. The Bradshaw Trail Road should not present a problem to most vehicles except for a few sandy stretches. Just keep moving in those areas. The 2.4 miles to the road's end and the center of Site A, however, is a different story. You probably will need four-wheel drive and high clearance to get all the way. If your vehicle can't make the trek, park and hike. You will find a lot of material along the way, but the best seems to be near the road's end. Look for orbicular geodes which tend to be filled with nice bubbly chalcedony, as well as very unusual petrified pine bark. The mines in the region were perlite mines and a few samples of that mineral might make nice display pieces in a mineral collection.

Site B, only a short distance farther west, boasts fine black agate, sagenite and occasional nodules and geodes. Excavations can be seen on the hillside as you approach the given mileage. To procure the best material it is necessary to do some digging but the work is relatively easy since the soil is soft. There are also a lot of chips and tumbling size pieces strewn all over, so, if you don't want to do any pick and shovel work, the site still may be of interest. Most of the little orbs are solid, having centers of banded agate, but a few do have crystalline- or chalcedony-filled interiors. Use good judgment when driving to Site A, since you must cross a sandy wash. If you are not sure whether or not your vehicle can get across, do not attempt it. Just park off the road and walk the short 0.4 miles to the diggings.

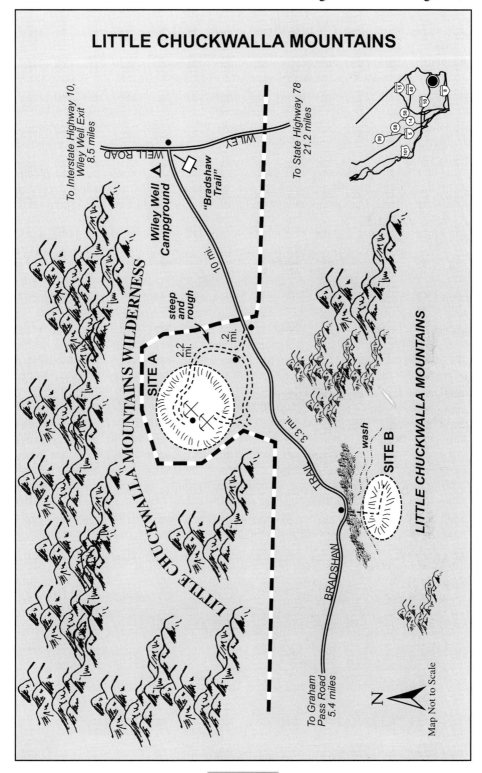

LITTLE CHUCKWALLA MOUNTAINS

To Interstate Highway 10, Wiley Well Exit 8.5 miles

WILEY WELL ROAD

Wiley Well Campground

"Bradshaw Trail"

To State Highway 78 21.2 miles

10 mi.

LITTLE CHUCKWALLA MOUNTAINS WILDERNESS

steep and rough

2.2 mi.

.2 mi.

SITE A

3.3 mi.

wash

SITE B

LITTLE CHUCKWALLA MOUNTAINS

BRADSHAW TRAIL

To Graham Pass Road 5.4 miles

N

Map Not to Scale

CHUCKWALLA WELL

Agate, jasper and chalcedony can be found throughout the hills and valleys on both sides of the Bradshaw Trail Road from where Graham Pass Road intersects continuing west to where Augustine Pass Road intersects. Stopping at random places along that stretch of road might prove fruitful, but, be advised that the concentrations are random which could make the effort somewhat frustrating. The sites discussed here are a little more reliable, even though they too have been picked over and do not provide the abundance they did a few decades ago.

The road to Chuckwalla Well, designated as Site A on the accompanying map, is approximately 3.2 miles west of where Graham Pass Road intersects the Bradshaw Trail. This location has long been known by Southern California rockhounds, and because of this, much of the best surface material has already been taken. There is still plenty of agate, jasper and petrified wood available if you are willing to do some hiking through the nearby hills and valleys. Just be patient and plan to spend some time. Material is most frequently found in areas of erosion, but it can also be picked up on the hillsides and even along the ruts leading in from the main road. Signs of digging can be seen on the hills to the north, and it might be productive to do some work in those areas. Most of the seams were worked out many years ago. DO NOT camp or park near Chuckwalla Well since it is an important watering spot for local wildlife! Occasionally, during dry weather periods, the BLM closes the road so local wildlife can have unhindered access to the life-giving water provided at the well. Please respect those closures and be satisfied with the plethora of other minerals that can be found nearby.

To get to Site B, return to the Bradshaw Trail, go west another 5.5 miles to Augustine Pass Road and turn right. This is a very rough route, and a rugged, high clearance vehicle will be needed to complete the journey. In fact, four-wheel drive might also be necessary in certain severely washed out places. Go about 1.5 miles to a fork and bear right, continuing approximately 0.6 miles farther. Throughout this final stretch, a lot of chalcedony and chalcedony-filled nodules can be found scattered all over, especially on the hill to the right, just past the fork. Some of the little orbs also contain tiny crystals, but such specimens are not very plentiful. Grossular garnet crystals can be obtained within the horizontal, greenish contact zone on the canyon wall, about 0.5 miles farther. Attack the deposit with hard rock tools in hopes of exposing a garnet-filled cavity.

The Road Entrance to the Collecting Spots

BLYTHE

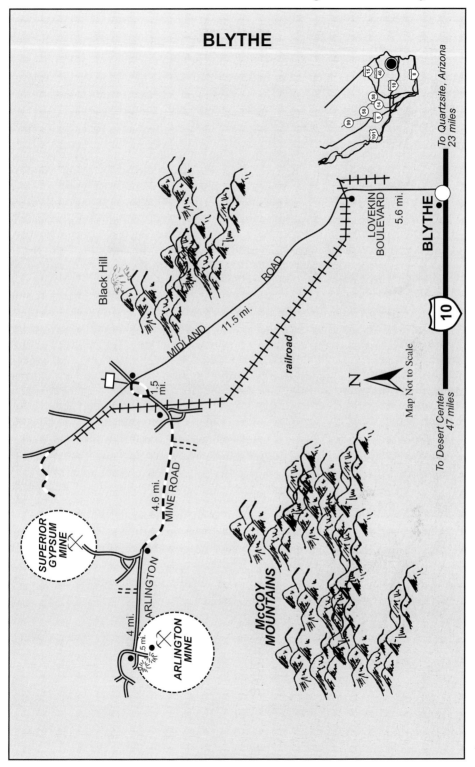

Black Hill

MIDLAND ROAD

11.5 mi.

railroad

LOVEKIN BOULEVARD

5.6 mi.

BLYTHE

10

To Quartzsite, Arizona 23 miles

To Desert Center 47 miles

N

Map Not to Scale

1.5 mi.

MINE ROAD

4.6 mi.

SUPERIOR GYPSUM MINE

ARLINGTON

4 mi.

.5 mi.

ARLINGTON MINE

McCOY MOUNTAINS

RED CLOUD JASPER

This location offers collectors an opportunity to pick up agate and some very colorful jasper, including highly-prized green and red bloodstone. It should be mentioned that access to the site is restricted, since it is in the proximity of Canyon Spring, an essential source of water for local wildlife. In fact, the BLM closes the region throughout the summer and well into the fall. It would be advisable to contact the governing BLM office to determine current status before making the long journey. That information can be obtained from: BLM Palm Springs Resource Area Office, 690 West Garnet Avenue, P.O. Box 581260, North Palm Springs, CA 92258; (760) 251-4800.

Be further advised that a substantial part of the trip will take you through a lot of very loose and deep sand, making four-wheel drive not only desirable, but probably essential. If at all possible, do not make this trip alone. When two or more vehicles travel together, if one gets stuck in the sand, the other can either go get help or tow the stuck one to more solid ground. Even with four-wheel drive, try not to stop in the sand—keep moving!

With all of that said, if you want to make the scenic trip, start by taking the Red Cloud/Summit Road Exit from Interstate Highway 10, about 35 miles east of Indio and 10 miles west of Desert Center. Proceed south. Stop at the BLM information bulletin board for current information. The bulletin board is located just off the pavement on Red Cloud/Summit Road. After leaving the pavement, the road has a very rough washboard surface, but it does smooth out a little farther along the way. At 2.3 miles, there is a three-way intersection. Proceed on County Road 41/Summit Road, which is the middle choice. After having gone a total of 10.6 miles, the Bradshaw Trail intersects and Summit Road ends. Bear right onto the Bradshaw Trail and follow it 4 more miles as it leads in and out of the treacherous sandy wash. At the given mileage is a BLM sign designating the right turn to Canyon Spring. Travel about 0.2 miles into the little canyon to where another BLM sign prohibits further vehicle travel. From there, park and walk north and west, searching the washes and surrounding landscape for agate and the colorful green and red jasper.

The Three-way Fork on the Way to Red Cloud

RED CLOUD

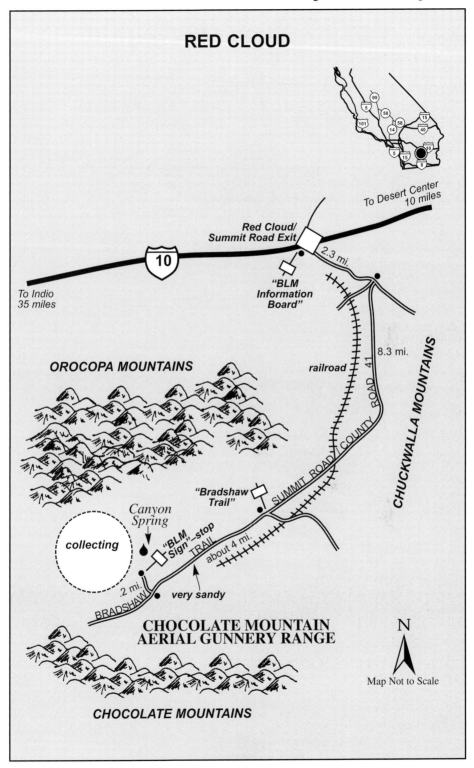

To Desert Center
10 miles

Red Cloud/
Summit Road Exit

10

2.3 mi.

"BLM
Information
Board"

To Indio
35 miles

OROCOPA MOUNTAINS

railroad

8.3 mi.

SUMMIT ROAD / COUNTY ROAD 41

CHUCKWALLA MOUNTAINS

"Bradshaw
Trail"

Canyon
Spring

collecting

"BLM
Sign"-stop
TRAIL

about 4 mi.

.2 mi.

BRADSHAW

very sandy

CHOCOLATE MOUNTAIN
AERIAL GUNNERY RANGE

N

Map Not to Scale

CHOCOLATE MOUNTAINS

OROCOPA MOUNTAINS FLUORITE

This location offers collectors some very nice and pleasantly colored specimens of fluorite. Colors include purple, yellow and green, as well as countless other shades. Some of the pieces possess more than one color or are even banded, those being real prizes for collectors. Such material, if solid enough, can be cut and polished. On the other hand, since fluorite is so soft, it is generally best suited for display or use in very low impact jewelry such as pins and bracelets.

This collecting site is centered around an old fluorspar mine situated on a hill overlooking a little canyon and it is right on the boundary of the new BLM administered Orocopa Mountains Wilderness Area. Be sure to read the restrictions governing these wilderness areas in the Introduction and take time to also read the BLM information at the bulletin board located where Red Canyon Trail intersects the pavement. Do not drive beyond any of the boundary markers, and if it appears that the collecting status at the old mine has changed, restrict yourself to regions below.

To get there, take the Chiriaco Summit Exit from Interstate Highway 10, about 27 miles east of Indio and 18 miles west of Desert Center. Proceed south to the frontage road and then go west, paralleling the interstate for 1.1 miles. The road to the collecting site is easy to spot due to the large BLM informational bulletin board at the intersection. Turn south onto SR 2013, which is Red Canyon Trail, and proceed 5.6 miles to where a steep and very rough little road leads right to the old fluorspar mine. Be sure to stay on SR 2013 for the entire journey. There are two major forks along the way, but there is also a BLM signpost at each helping to sort out which direction to proceed.

Drive as far toward the little mine as you safely can and park. The road gets extremely steep and treacherous and there is virtually no place to turn around once you commit toward the summit. Don't think that four-wheel drive will make it any safer—it won't. Hike up the old road or in the wash that runs along its side to the top of the hill. Explore the pits and surrounding terrain for the fluorite.

It should be mentioned that the General Patton Museum is located on the north side of Interstate Highway 10 at Chiriaco Summit. The address is 62510 Chiriaco Road, Chiriaco Summit, CA 92201. For hours or more information, call (760) 227-3483. It might be an interesting place to visit if you have the time. Information and relics left from when he was training soldiers for desert warfare in this region are exhibited in the museum, and provide a unique bit of American history few people know about.

OROCOPA MOUNTAINS

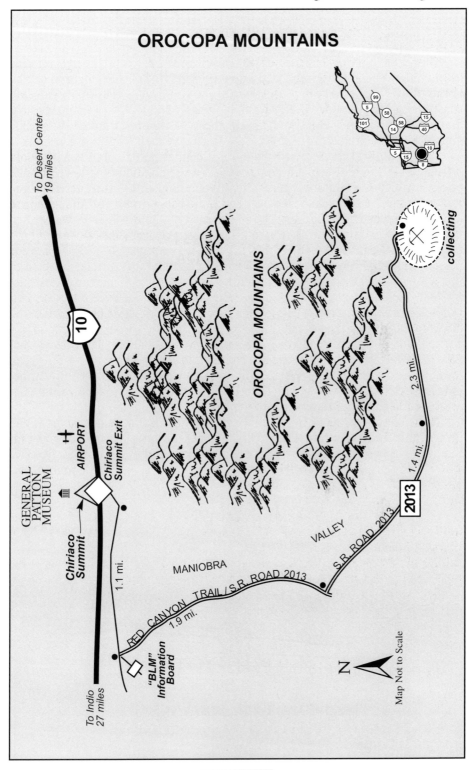

collecting

To Desert Center
19 miles

10

2.3 mi.

OROCOPA MOUNTAINS

1.4 mi.

AIRPORT

Chiriaco
Summit Exit

GENERAL
PATTON
MUSEUM

Chiriaco
Summit

2013

S.R. ROAD 2013

VALLEY

1.1 mi.

MANIOBRA

RED CANYON TRAIL / S.R. ROAD 2013

1.9 mi.

To Indio
27 miles

"BLM"
Information
Board

N

Map Not to Scale

VIDAL JUNCTION

The desert lands surrounding the large wash illustrated on the accompanying map have long been known for the fine chalcedony that can be found there. At one time, this locality was virtually covered with the sometimes sizable and perfectly formed "roses." Now, they are considerably more difficult to find, but still available to those willing to spend some time and do a little hiking.

To get there, take U.S. Highway 95 for 9.7 miles north from Vidal Junction. At that point, the highway crosses the wash, and you should park well off the pavement before beginning your search. Some faint ruts can be seen leading east through the sand, and, if you have four-wheel drive, you may want to drive instead of walk. Be very cautious, though. The sand is quite deep in places, and even four-wheel drive vehicles may have problems. This would not be a good location to get stuck.

The best collecting seems to be toward the mountains, primarily north of the wash, well away from the pavement. Go at least 1 mile to where the collecting tends to get much better. Once you get to a promising spot, just randomly roam the area, keeping an eye out for the easily spotted, white and pink "roses."

Generally, the chalcedony can be found just about anywhere from U.S. Highway 95, extending east all the way to the foothills about 5.5 miles away. It is unusual, but some places are virtually void of the chalcedony, while, only a short distance farther, the desert pavement might be loaded with it. The bright white color makes it very easy to spot.

Remember that this is an arid and desolate region. Take extra water. If you choose to hike away from the highway, do not lose your bearings or go so far that it might be very difficult or impossible to get back.

Looking for Chalcedony at the Collecting Site

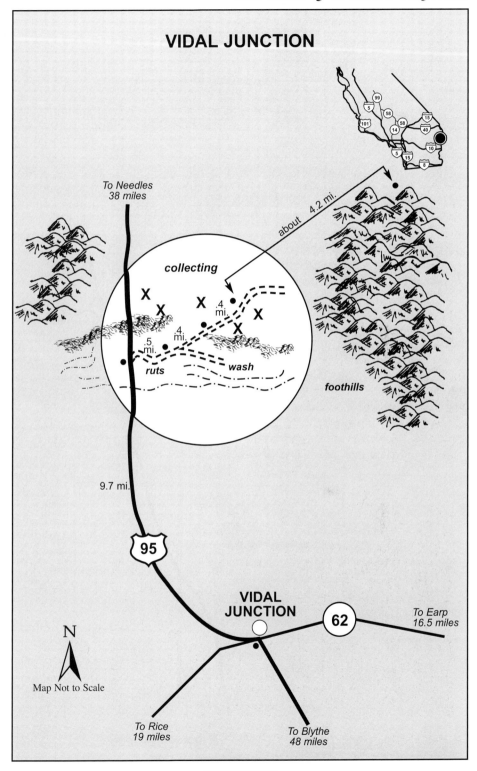

VIDAL JUNCTION

To Needles
38 miles

about 4.2 mi.

collecting

X
X
X
X
X
X

.4 mi.

.4 mi.

.5 mi.

ruts

wash

foothills

9.7 mi.

95

VIDAL
JUNCTION

62

To Earp
16.5 miles

N

Map Not to Scale

To Rice
19 miles

To Blythe
48 miles

BIG RIVER

These two locations provide the collector with a good selection of jasper and agate, as well as pieces of bright white bubbly chalcedony. To get to Site A, the least productive of the two, go west from Earp 1.5 miles, and then turn north onto the dirt road. Continue 4 miles to a fork, where you should bear right another 0.4 miles toward the conspicuous little hill. The road is severely washed out for the last 0.2 miles and most vehicles will not be able to make it all the way.

Much of the jasper found here is grainy and incapable of taking a polish, some are outstanding. There is a lot of tan, orange, red and yellow material, with a few pieces displaying beautiful swirls of color. The prize is the rainbow variety, consisting of vivid, multicolored bands which can be used to make incredibly beautiful polished pieces.

Site B offers far greater quantities and a more consistently higher quality. It is reached by returning to the pavement, going west another 2.6 miles and then heading north. The turnoff is just east of where the power lines cross. The best way to find the road is to simply head north from the pavement at the given mileage, and after rising over the little ridge, the ruts will easily be seen.

The collecting extends for quite a distance throughout the surrounding hills on both sides of the road, and if you allow enough time and are willing to do some walking, this locality could provide a considerable quantity of outstanding specimens. Site B offers agate, brilliant red jasper, mottled jasper and jasp-agate. The agate occurs in many colors and patterns, with the most sought after being a delicately banded fortification variety.

The entire terrain between Site A and Site B affords a lot of collecting potential. If you have the time and energy, it might prove very fruitful to do some random exploration on your own. Just be careful not to lose your bearings, or walk too far. Take some water and other supplies, and try to avoid visiting during the scorching summer months.

Parked at the Collecting Site

BIG RIVER

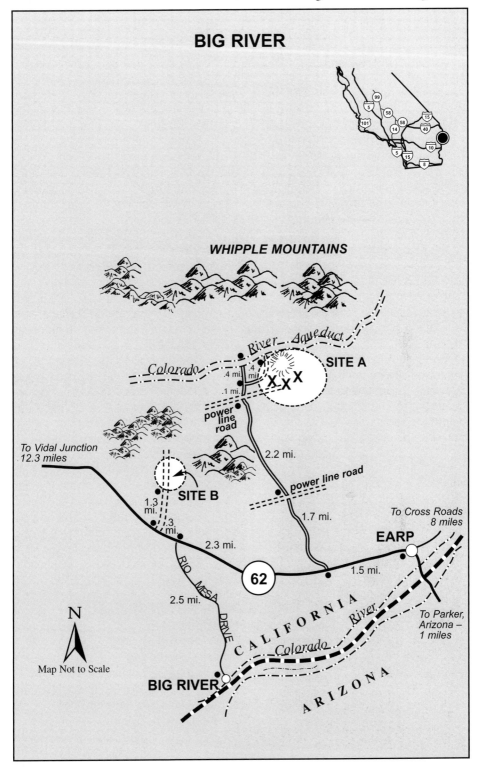

WHIPPLE MOUNTAINS

Colorado River Aqueduct

.4 mi.

.4 mi.

SITE A

X X X

.1 mi.

power line road

2.2 mi.

To Vidal Junction
12.3 miles

SITE B

1.3 mi.

power line road

.3 mi.

1.7 mi.

To Cross Roads
8 miles

EARP

2.3 mi.

62

1.5 mi.

RIO MESA DRIVE

2.5 mi.

CALIFORNIA

Colorado River

To Parker,
Arizona –
1 miles

N

Map Not to Scale

BIG RIVER

ARIZONA

TURTLE MOUNTAINS

Much of the region surrounding the scenic Turtle Mountains is now protected as a BLM Wilderness Area. The approved roads are well-marked, as are the boundaries, and you should familiarize yourself with the regulations governing those localities as discussed in the Introduction. Specific information related to each of the sites shown on the map are discussed below.

Regions surrounding the Turtle Mountains have long been known for the beautiful chalcedony roses and agate that have been found there. Just about anywhere you choose to explore near that spectacular desert mountain range offers great collecting potential. The sites described here are definitely not the only ones in the area and the locality has been well-known amongst mineral collectors for decades. Subsequently, this makes it tougher and tougher to find larger specimens, especially near the main roads. For that reason some random exploration might prove to be fun, as well as productive.

To get to Site A, take Turtle Mountain Road west from U.S. Highway 95. After driving 6 miles, and extending at least another 4.3 miles, you can stop just about anywhere and roam the countryside on either side of the road looking for nice agate and chalcedony roses. Site A is not in the Turtle Mountains Wilderness Area.

After having gone 10.3 miles from U.S. Highway 95, stay on the main road, bearing right 2 more miles to where an old road can be spotted going left. Proceed south 1.5 miles, turn right and park at the wilderness boundary marker. This final stretch is not in the wilderness area, but it is right on the eastern boundary. From where you park, hike west into the wilderness to Site B, located a little less than half-mile from the road that leads south from the main one. This is often referred to as Agate Hill, and on and around that little mountain you can find occasional geodes and nodules, as well as fortification and dendritic agate.

Back on the main road, go another for 1.8 miles to where the road crosses a wash. Park well off the roadway and hike north about 0.2 miles to Chalcedony Hill, Site C, on the left. A lot of "roses" can be found there, some quite sizable. This location is not in the wilderness area.

Site D is reached by doubling back 3.8 miles and going right (south) toward the mountains. Drive 1 mile, bear left 0.3 miles, and then left again to a wash, 0.2 miles farther. The ruts leading that final 0.2 miles may be closed by the BLM thereby requiring you to walk to the wash. Beautiful chalcedony, jasper and agate can be found throughout the surrounding terrain. This location is not in the wilderness area.

Site E is extensive, and boasts a lot of chalcedony, agate and jasper, but most is somewhat small. If you are willing to walk a distance from the road, there is still plenty of good material available. This spot is right on the wilderness boundary. You can hike as far into the wilderness as you like, but cannot drive.

Road Leading into the Collecting Area

TURTLE MOUNTAINS

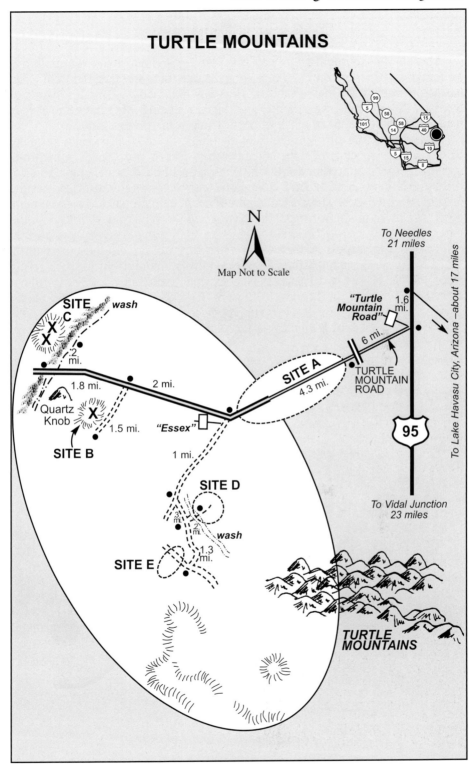

N

Map Not to Scale

*To Needles
21 miles*

SITE
C

wash

X
X

.2.
mi.

1.8 mi.

2 mi.

Quartz
Knob

1.5 mi.

X

SITE B

"Essex"

SITE A

4.3 mi.

**"Turtle
Mountain
Road"**

1.6
mi.

6 mi.

TURTLE
MOUNTAIN
ROAD

To Lake Havasu City, Arizona –about 17 miles

95

1 mi.

SITE D

.3
mi.

.2
mi.

wash

SITE E

1.3
mi.

*To Vidal Junction
23 miles*

**TURTLE
MOUNTAINS**

LAKE HAVASU

This site has a little hill that contains some agate and jasper, in a multitude of patterns and color combinations. To get there, take the Lake Havasu Road east from where it intersects U.S. Highway 95, about 21 miles south of Needles. Go 12.4 miles and then follow the ruts leading off to the south as they head for the little mountain of agate, about 1 mile from the pavement.

Please note that this site has been available for over fifty years, so many of the prized specimens have already been picked out. Some worthwhile specimens can still be found, but only with a lot of hard work. In addition, in the surrounding area to this claim, one can obtain interesting brecciated jasper, colorful opalite and a lot of chalcedony. The quality all tends to be quite good, but there is still a considerable variation, so take time to find only the best.

To get the largest pieces, it is necessary to attack the hill with a sledgehammer, chisels, pry bars, gads and gloves. Simply start to work at any place you feel shows particularly good color and quality, being very careful not to fracture what you are trying to remove. It is also essential that you wear goggles when striking the easily splintered agate and jasper. Needle-like slivers of stone are often sent flying through the air and they could severely damage an uncovered eye.

This is a private claim held by the Needles Gem & Mineral Society and to visit, you have to be a member or be accompanied by a one. To contact the society, call (760) 326-5005 or (760) 326-1148. Their address is 251 Mustang Lane, Needles, CA 92365.

Little Hill Composed of Agate and Jasper

LAKE HAVASU

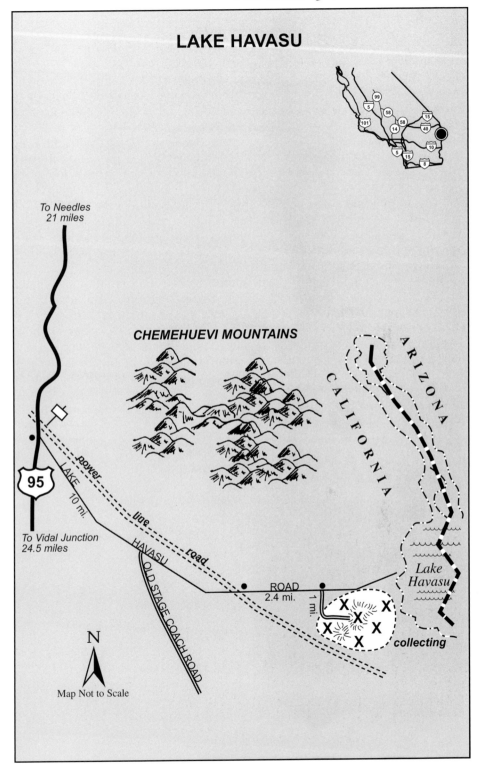

To Needles
21 miles

CHEMEHUEVI MOUNTAINS

ARIZONA

CALIFORNIA

95

To Vidal Junction
24.5 miles

power

LAKE
10 mi.

line
road

HAVASU

OLD STAGE COACH ROAD

ROAD
2.4 mi.

1 mi.

Lake
Havasu

X X
X
X X
X

collecting

N

Map Not to Scale

DANBY

Danby is best-known amongst rockhounds as a reliable source of very colorful opalite. In addition collectors can find small amounts of orpiment, realgar, sphalerite, malachite, chrysocolla, agate, jasper and chalcedony throughout the region. To get to the opalite deposit, labeled Site A on the map, go west from Essex on the National Trails Highway for 9.1 miles to Danby Road. From there, turn south and proceed 1.6 miles, cross the railroad tracks, and then bear right alongside the tracks another 6.6 miles away. At the given mileage, go left half-mile to the little mounds and fire rings, those marking the opalite deposit.

A lot of specimens can be picked up from the ground, especially near the pits. The largest and best pieces are obtained by digging with a pick and shovel into the soft sand. The opalite occurs in a wide variety of colors, some containing interesting moss-like inclusions. Be sure to sample material from throughout the deposit, since the colors vary greatly from pit to pit.

Site B, which is actually a small dump, can be seen from the road shown on the map. There, you should be able to find orpiment and realgar, the colorful orange and red ores of arsenic. Because of the arsenic content, it is imperative that you be careful when handling specimens and be certain to wash your hands after gathering samples. On the dumps at Site C, one can find fluorescent opalite, some of which contains metallic sphalerite. Since both Sites B and C are on mine dumps, there is a possibility that there could be restrictions related to collecting. If there is any indication that the associated mining operations are active or currently under a valid claim, do not collect there without first seeking permission.

Site D boasts malachite and chrysocolla, but most is either stained or very grainy and thereby incapable of taking a polish. Some of the more sizable pieces are nice for display. While in the area, be sure to take time to inspect any of the washes for agate, jasper, chalcedony, malachite and chrysocolla.

Selection of Opalite
Found Near Danby

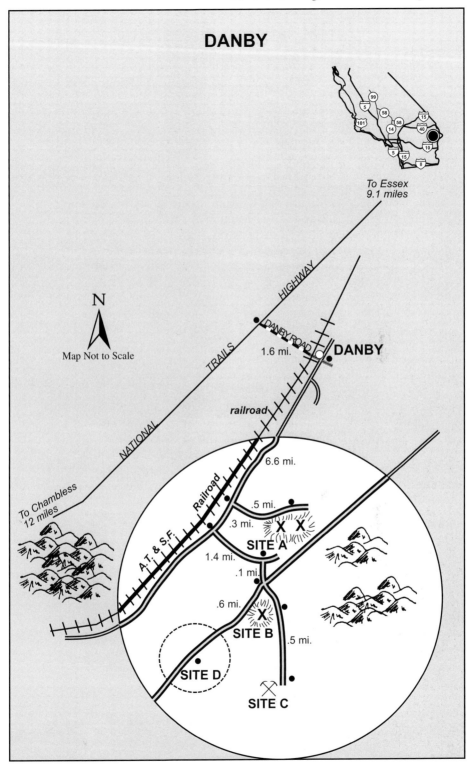

DANBY

To Essex
9.1 miles

N
Map Not to Scale

To Chambless
12 miles

HIGHWAY

TRAILS

NATIONAL

DANBY ROAD

1.6 mi.

DANBY

railroad

Railroad

A.T. & S.F.

6.6 mi.

.5 mi.

.3 mi.

X   X
SITE A

1.4 mi.

.1 mi.

.6 mi.

X
SITE B

.5 mi.

SITE D

SITE C

CADIZ

Colorful red marble and interesting fossilized trilobites can be found in and around an old abandoned quarry, just south of the Marble Mountains. To get there from Chambless on the National Trails Highway (old Route 66), take Cadiz Road south 2.2 miles to where some dim tracks can be seen intersecting from the east. If you get to where the paved road makes a sharp turn, as shown on the map, you have gone too far and should double back after about 0.1 miles. Follow the rough dirt road 2 miles and then turn left onto the ruts leading toward the cliffs another 0.8 miles to where you should park.

From the parking spot at the base of the hill, there is a trail leading to the reddish brown trilobite-bearing shale. Choose what you feel is a promising spot and use a hammer and chisel to remove as big a chunk of the shale as possible. Then, CAREFULLY split it along any of the bedding planes with a sturdy knife, in hopes of exposing a reddish brown trilobite. It takes a lot of patience, luck and skill to obtain complete specimens, but with practice, you should develop the technique. Once you discover part of a trilobite, you must work very carefully to expose what remains with a small ice pick or knife.

It is debatable which requires more patience, finding the fossils in the first place, or once found, uncovering them without doing any damage. Be advised that complete trilobites are few and far between. This particular species decomposed rapidly, and frequently "broke up" before being cemented in stone. Even partial specimens are nice, so don't let that discourage you.

If you continue along the trail, it ends at a marble quarry. Much of the beautiful reddish-brown marble found there is quite solid and capable of taking a nice polish. Marble is best used for larger pieces, such as bookends, carvings and clock faces, but some, if it displays nice color contrast, can be used for cabochons. The quality varies considerably throughout the deposit. Look for pieces with the best color and least graininess. This quarry has been abandoned for years, but if there is any sign that is no longer the case, be sure to seek permission to collect.

The Collecting Area

CADIZ

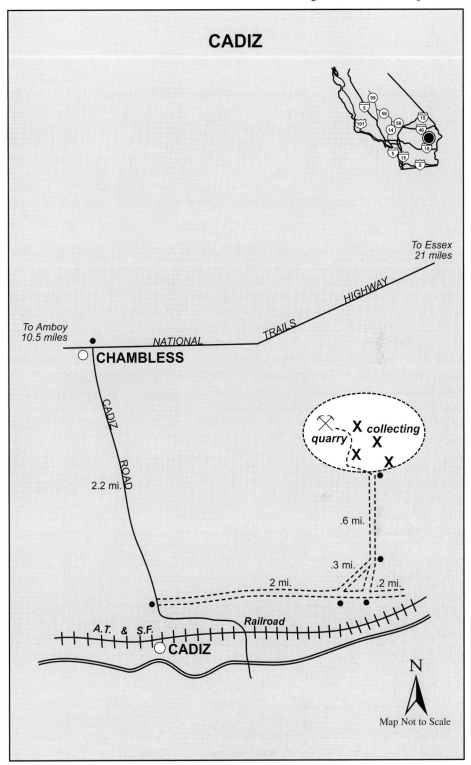

To Essex
21 miles

HIGHWAY

TRAILS

NATIONAL

To Amboy
10.5 miles

CHAMBLESS

CADIZ ROAD

2.2 mi.

X collecting

quarry

X

X

X

X

.6 mi.

.3 mi.

2 mi.

.2 mi.

Railroad

A.T. & S.F.

CADIZ

N

Map Not to Scale

CHAMBLESS

Much of the region in and around the Marble Mountains is now protected from vehicle traffic by its inclusion within the Trilobite Wilderness Area. BLM approved roads and boundaries are well-marked, and you should familiarize yourself with the regulations governing those localities by reading the data provided in the Introduction. Specific details related to each of the Chambless sites are discussed below.

Hematite, magnetite, garnet, epidote, marble and fossils can all be found in the Marble Mountains just north of Chambless. To get to the base of the mountains, go 0.3 miles west from Cadiz Road on the National Trails Highway and then follow Mactull Avenue half-mile to a house on the left. Jog around that house and continue north another 1.4 miles. The road deteriorates greatly as you enter the foothills, and a rugged, high clearance vehicle is advisable. At the given mileage, bear left another 0.3 miles to the remnants of an old iron mine designated as Site A. Be advised that this mine lies directly on the southern boundary of the wilderness area. Do not drive beyond the boundary marker.

It is also important to note that there are many roads in this region and not all are shown on the map. If you pay attention to the mileage and the surrounding landscape, there should be no major problem. The iron deposit can easily be spotted a few tenths of a mile past where you must park. It might be tempting to try to drive all the way to the old mine if you have four-wheel drive but that could prove to be very foolish. Most of the rocks at Site A are covered with a reddish-brown crust concealing their often spectacular inclusions of bright hematite and magnetite. For that reason it is necessary to split all suspect stones with a sledgehammer to reveal the non-oxidized and often spectacularly beautiful interiors.

Only a short distance northeast of the iron mine is an old quarry filled with limestone and marble. Much of the marble takes a good polish and sizable chunks can be found there. If you want to explore the quarry, it is necessary to walk, but it could be worth the effort.

Site B is generally regarded to be the favorite of the Marble Mountain locations. There has been sporadic exploratory mining there during the past decade, so if there are indications of current work or valid claims protecting the deposit, do not collect without first getting permission to do so. Here, among other things, is a tiny mountain of garnet. The dark red and brown crystals are massed together, and chunks of the crystal clusters are great for display in a mineral collection. In addition, a lot of bright green epidote is scattered about, and much is filled with brilliant, metallic hematite. The lime-green epidote, filled with metallic hematite, is extremely showy and highly-prized for display in a mineral collection. There is also some red hematite, drusy quartz and calcite crystals to be found throughout Site B, but none of these minerals are overly plentiful. Site B is situated within the Trilobite Wilderness Area, so you must park at the wilderness boundary marker and hike the approximate 0.5 additional miles to the old diggings. Don't despair, though. A lot of nice material can be found near where you must park probably making it unnecessary to make that final uphill trek.

Farther east is Site C, situated in a little canyon. At the given mileage is a grayish ridge of limestone within which are a lot of interesting fossils. Site C is just north of the wilderness boundary, but the short walk is not bad.

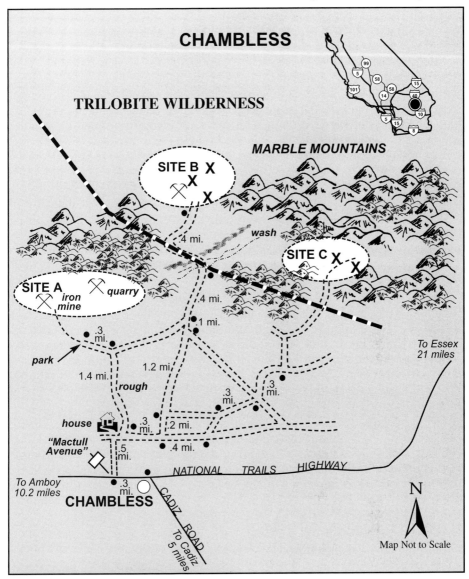

CHAMBLESS

TRILOBITE WILDERNESS

MARBLE MOUNTAINS

SITE B

SITE C

SITE A
iron
mine   quarry

wash

.4 mi.

.4 mi.

.1 mi.

park

.3 mi.

1.2 mi.

1.4 mi.

rough

.3 mi.

house

.3 mi.

.2 mi.

"Mactull Avenue"

.5 mi.

.4 mi.

NATIONAL TRAILS HIGHWAY

To Essex 21 miles

To Amboy 10.2 miles

.3 mi.

CHAMBLESS

CADIZ ROAD

To Cadiz 5 miles

N

Map Not to Scale

Parked at Site B in the Marble Mountains Near Chambless

ORANGE BLOSSOM COPPER

Both of the locations discussed here are situated on and around old mine dumps. If either of them appear to no longer be abandoned do not collect there without first gaining permission to do so. Be very careful when at an old mine since there can be broken glass, nails, rotten shaft and uncovered pits.

Good pieces of purple dumortierite and a lot of colorful copper ores can be found along the Kelbaker Road between Route 66 and Interstate Highway 40. To get to Site A, an old mine where rockhounds can procure occasional pieces of the somewhat rare mineral dumortierite, take Kelbaker Road 3.5 miles north from The National Trails Highway (Route 66). At that point, turn left onto the rough dirt tracks heading toward the hills. Go only 0.4 miles to the old mine and simply dig through its dumps in search of the colorful purple cutting material. It is sometimes helpful to split suspect rocks, in hopes of exposing otherwise concealed dumortierite. A lot of what is found here is quite soft, but it will still take an considerable amount of time to do some digging in order to find the best this spot has to offer.

The copper ores are found in regions surrounding the old Orange Blossom Mine, designated as Site B on the map. That location is reached by returning to Kelbaker Road and proceeding north another 6.5 miles. From there, go left 3.9 miles and then right another 2.3 miles to a fork. It is necessary to cross a sandy wash along the way, so be certain your vehicle can make it across. If you turn right at the fork, the road leads to a smaller portion of the Orange Blossom Mine where some specimens can be obtained. The best collecting is in and around the main dumps, accessed by bearing left another half-mile.

Those dumps contain blue chrysocolla and malachite stained rock. Most is no more than a brilliantly colored stain, but some of the chrysocolla-filled fissures and cavities are thick enough to be cut and polished. Even when in combination with the host rock can be used to make very nice cabochons.

There is no special secret to collecting here. Simply search through the dumps for the easily spotted bright blue chrysocolla or green malachite. A hand rake or trowel will prove useful for light digging into the dumps. If you feel like doing some heavy work, a pick and shovel will surely expose more material, thereby increasing your chances for finding bigger and better specimens.

ORANGE BLOSSOM

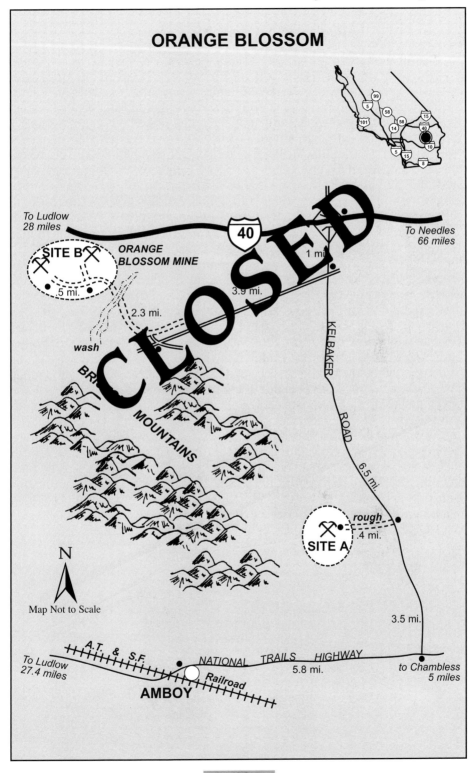

To Ludlow
28 miles

To Needles
66 miles

40

1 mi.

SITE B

ORANGE BLOSSOM MINE

.5 mi.

3.9 mi.

2.3 mi.

wash

KELBAKER ROAD

6.5 mi.

BR MOUNTAINS

rough

.4 mi.

SITE A

N

Map Not to Scale

3.5 mi.

A.T. & S.F.

NATIONAL TRAILS HIGHWAY

To Ludlow
27.4 miles

5.8 mi.

to Chambless
5 miles

Railroad

AMBOY

CLOSED

KELBAKER ROAD

Beautiful chalcedony roses, occasional geodes and nodules can be found at the two sites depicted on the accompanying map. To get to Site B, go west on the National Trails Highway about 5 miles from Chambless and turn north onto Kelbaker Road. Travel 1.5 miles to where some dim ruts can be seen leading east into the desert pavement. It should be noted that Site B is not actually a specific spot, but more the center of a region. Travel on the ruts only about 0.1 miles and then go north on the desert pavement, stopping just about anywhere for quite a distance to look for nice and well formed chalcedony roses. Most are white, but a few beautiful light pink specimens can be also obtained. Size ranges from very tiny to some measuring many inches across. The roses are very easy to spot, contrasting vividly against the dark desert pavement. If you allow plenty of time here, and are willing to do some walking, the potential is very good for finding real beauties. Since this is primarily a surface deposit, the supply tends to become more and more depleted each year as collecting continues. This makes it necessary to get to the less accessible portions of the extensive desert pavement area to find the best and most sizable roses. For those willing to make the effort, there is still much to be found.

To get to Site A, which is about 1 mile within the boundaries of the Trilobite Wilderness Area, return to Kelbaker Road. From there drive 5.7 miles farther north to where a road leads off to the east. Go about 0.3 miles to the wilderness boundary marker, park, and then prepare to hike about 1 mile. Take something to drink, digging tools and a sturdy bag or backpack for carrying specimens and equipment. Follow the old road to the conspicuous brown hills which designate the edge of the collecting site.

Near the brown hills you can dig for geodes and nodules, but only a few have crystal centers. Look throughout the flatlands surrounding the hill for chalcedony, especially across the ravine to the south. The agate-filled nodules from this location are nice, but not overly plentiful. It takes a lot of digging with pick and shovel and a substantial amount of luck to find much. Other deposits are reported to be farther in, so it might be worth your time to do some additional exploration, if you have the time and energy.

Searching for
Chalcedony Roses
at Site B

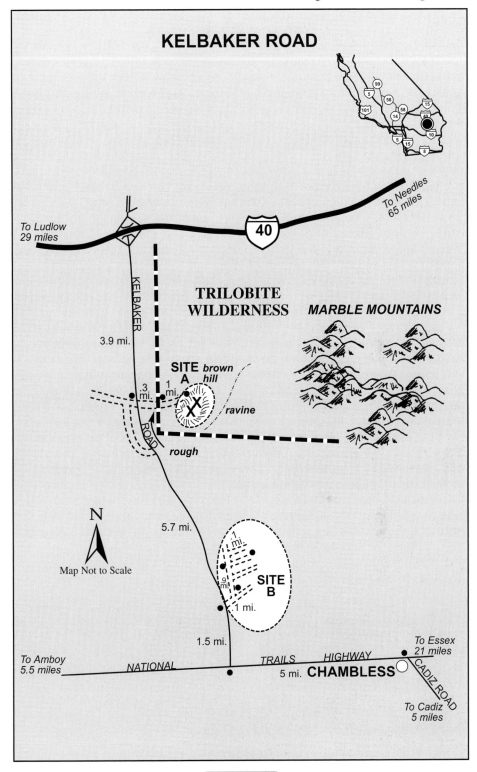

KELBAKER ROAD

To Needles
65 miles

To Ludlow
29 miles

40

KELBAKER

3.9 mi.

**TRILOBITE
WILDERNESS**

MARBLE MOUNTAINS

**SITE
A** *brown
hill*

.3.
mi.

1
mi.

ravine

ROAD

rough

N

Map Not to Scale

5.7 mi.

1
mi.

.9
mi.

**SITE
B**

.1 mi.

1.5 mi.

To Essex
21 miles

To Amboy
5.5 miles

NATIONAL   *TRAILS*   *HIGHWAY*

5 mi. **CHAMBLESS**

CADIZ ROAD

To Cadiz
5 miles

LUDLOW MINERALS

Site A consists of a colossal obsidian field, boasting virtually limitless amounts of that often beautiful volcanic glass, even though most is not gem quality, being somewhat porous. Site B offers agate, jasper and chalcedony.

To get to Site A, the Ludlow Obsidian Field, drive about 50 miles east of Barstow and take the Ludlow Exit from Interstate Highway 40. From there, go south a very short distance to the National Trails Highway, (old Route 66) where you should turn left (east). Proceed about 1.5 miles to the easily spotted obsidian deposit and find a good place to pull off the road. Explore the land south of the railroad tracks. Plan to do some walking and be willing to allow sufficient time to locate the best of what this location has to offer.

It seems that the smaller pieces tend to be of higher quality, but boulders can sometimes also be nice. Most are jet black, while some tend to be gray. It is tempting to drive through the field in an effort to get to more remote and, hopefully, less picked-over regions. It is strongly recommended that you resist that temptation since the hilly, deep sand makes travel treacherous, even in a four-wheel drive vehicle.

To get to Site B, continue east on the National Trails Highway another 7.8 miles to a point just before the road turns to the southeast. On your right, at the given mileage, will be a very difficult to spot road leading off the pavement. If you miss the turn on your first try and have to double back, be very careful when doing so since cars travel very fast on this remote highway. When you get onto the old dirt road, proceed 0.6 miles to a fork, that designating the center of Site B. There is a nice flat place to camp, if you want to spend the night. Collecting takes place on the upper regions, as well as along the right fork as it goes down to the old mining area. Look near and in the orangish rock for agate, especially prized carnelian. There is also chalcedony and occasional chunks of jasper scattered about so don't neglect searching for those other nice cutting materials also.

Remember that this is an arid desert location and it is suggested that you take something to drink, especially if you plan to hike any distance. Carry a heavy-duty collecting bag, and, if you plan to split any of the obsidian with a rock hammer, be sure to wear gloves and goggles. The sharp slivers are often sent streaking through the air when struck! Limited supplies and gasoline are available in nearby Ludlow.

The Road to Ludlow

LUDLOW

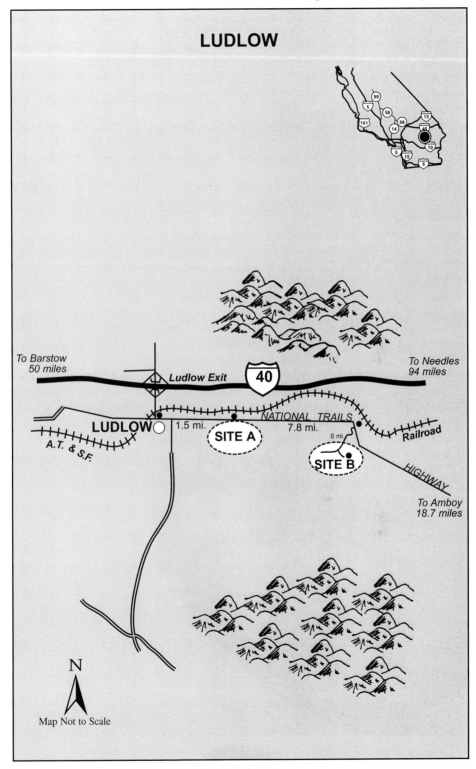

To Barstow
50 miles

To Needles
94 miles

Ludlow Exit

40

NATIONAL TRAILS

LUDLOW

1.5 mi.

SITE A

7.8 mi.

.6 mi.

SITE B

Railroad

HIGHWAY

A.T. & S.F.

To Amboy
18.7 miles

N

Map Not to Scale

CADY MOUNTAINS

The Cady Mountains, situated about 50 miles east of Barstow, have offered rockhounds a wide variety of extremely colorful cutting materials and other minerals for decades. In spite of the locality's popularity, there is still plenty to be found.

To get there, take the Ludlow Exit from Interstate Highway 40, go north, away from town, and then follow the pavement as it turns west. There are some rough stretches of road, occasional deep sand and numerous washouts throughout the area, so don't go where your vehicle isn't designed to go.

Site A features a tiny hill just east of the road which is covered with an amazing variety of colorful jasper. Most is layered, in tones of brown and black, but collectors can also find specimens in shades of green, red and orange, in an infinite variety of designs and color combinations.

Rhombohedral calcite crystals fill the cracks and cavities in the easily spotted contact zone, high on the hill at Site B. Be careful when climbing since the hill is steep and the soil is somewhat loose. Tiny, interesting calcite bubbles can be found filling the voids in rocks lying in the wash a short distance west of the hill.

Brilliant red, yellow and yellow-green hills mark Site C. The bright colors are a result of the huge amounts of jasper lying on the surface. The hill farthest south seems to have the best quality and most vivid colors, but all are remarkable. Take time to pick out only the most solid, since much of what can be found here is decomposing.

The road to Site D is sandy and rough, so four-wheel drive is highly recommended. Travel to the road's end, park and hike about 0.25 miles to where seams of rhombohedral calcite crystals can be spotted running through the canyon walls. In addition, look for small chunks of chalcedony and agate throughout the wash leading to the calcite.

More jasper, chalcedony and very nice agate can be found throughout the hills at Site E, and the mine dumps at Site F afford interesting slag, which can be used to make unusual display pieces. Site G offers a good selection of jasper, agate and chalcedony in a variety of colors and patterns, scattered throughout the terrain.

Site D

CADY MOUNTAINS

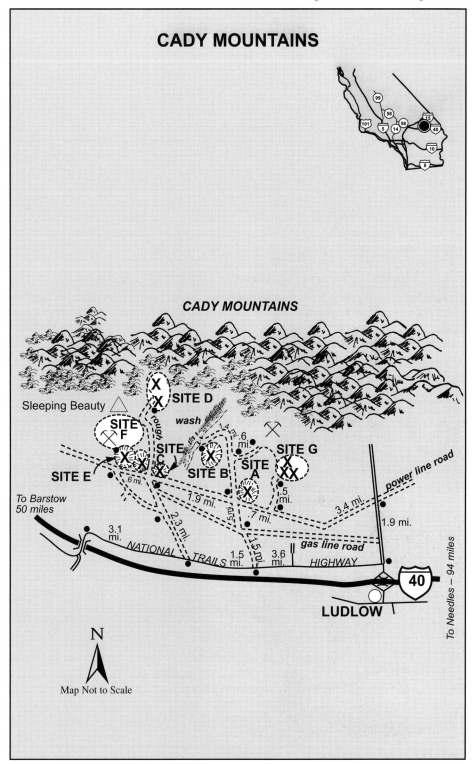

CADY MOUNTAINS

Sleeping Beauty

SITE D

wash

SITE F

rough

SITE C

SITE E

SITE B

SITE A

SITE G

.6 mi.

.4 mi.

.6 mi.

.5 mi.

.5 mi.

1.9 mi.

.7 mi.

3.4 mi.

power line road

1.9 mi.

gas line road

To Barstow 50 miles

3.1 mi.

2.3 mi.

1.3 mi.

NATIONAL TRAILS

1.5 mi.

3.6 mi.

HIGHWAY

40

LUDLOW

To Needles – 94 miles

N

Map Not to Scale

BRISTOL MOUNTAINS ONYX

This site is nestled about 2 miles into the new BLM supervised Bristol Mountains Wilderness Area. Collecting is allowed at the site, but you can no longer drive to the old onyx mine, which marks the center of the collecting. The hike from the wilderness boundary is about 2 miles, tending to be uphill most of the way. BLM approved roads are well-marked, as are the boundaries, and you should familiarize yourself with the regulations governing those localities as discussed in the Introduction. Obviously, this location is only for people in excellent health and should not be attempted during the hot summer months.

In addition to the 2 mile hike, the trip to the parking spot should only be attempted in a four-wheel drive vehicle. The road goes over some rough terrain, as well as through many sandy washes.

If you do choose to make this most challenging trip, you will be able to get some extremely colorful onyx, as well as good specimens of jasper. To get there, start in Ludlow, which is just south of Interstate Highway 40 and about 50 miles east of Barstow. Go north, pass under Interstate Highway 40, and continue north onto the dirt road at the point where the National Trails Highway makes a sharp turn to the left, as shown on the map. After having gone 1.9 miles you will intersect a power line road, and it is there where you turn to the right. Follow that road east, as it approximately parallels the power lines and skirts the northern edge of the wilderness area. Once you have traveled 13.2 miles, there will be some rough tracks leading off to the south. Follow that road about 0.1 miles to the wilderness boundary marker where you should park and commence the hike. Be certain to take plenty of water as well as a sturdy backpack or collecting bag to haul specimens and tools.

At the road's end, about 2.1 miles from you had to park, is the center of the collecting site. It is easy to spot where the earlier miners had quarried the beautiful onyx. This is where you should begin your search. The material of primary interest here is called Strawberry Onyx, due to its reddish-pink color. The hues are often vivid and the swirls and bands pronounced. This, in fact, is some of the best onyx to originate from the Mojave Desert. The only reason the mine couldn't make a profit was due to the expense of getting it back to "civilization."

There is a lot of already broken up material lying throughout the mine area and lower slopes, and because of wilderness regulations, you should be satisfied with what has already been broken free from the deposit. In addition, there is a lot of jasper, especially on and around the little hill just west of the quarry. This is not a well-known collecting location, partly due to its relative inaccessibility. There is a lot to be found, if you are willing to spend the time. Just don't lose your bearings, since this is not a spot where you would want to get lost.

BRISTOL MOUNTAINS

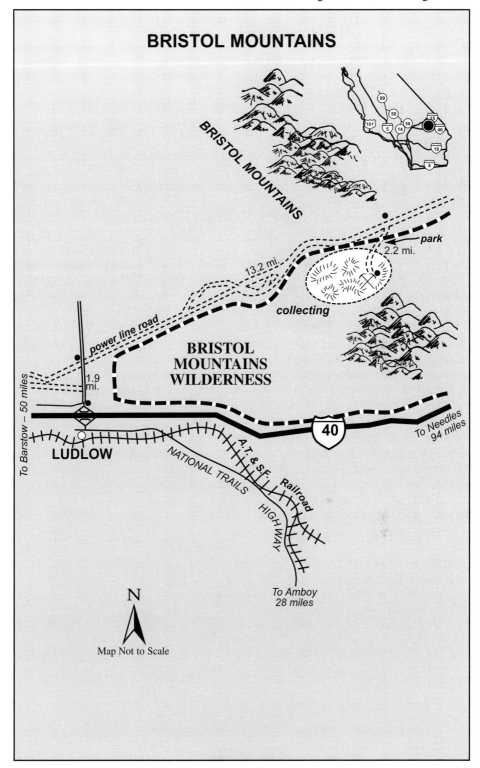

BROADWELL DRY LAKE

The three sites illustrated on the accompanying map provide collectors with a nice variety of minerals. Be cautious, when traveling through the region since the roads go through a lot of deep sand and there are a number of washouts along the way. Four-wheel drive is highly recommended, but may not be necessary. Heavy-duty, high clearance trucks should be able to get through.

To get to Site A, take the Ludlow Exit from Interstate Highway 40, which is about 50 miles east of Barstow, and head north for 7.6 miles. Instead of following the pavement, as it bears to the west, you should proceed straight ahead onto the dirt tracks. The final 0.2 miles is extremely rough, and you may be forced to hike that final stretch, even if you have four-wheel drive. Use good judgment as to where you should park, and don't take chances in this somewhat desolate desert region. The road terminates at a large wash where one can find chalcedony and a lot of top quality agate. This includes beautiful flame and lace varieties. Pieces of common opal can also be picked up, in colors ranging from pink and white to prize violet. For those wanting to do sledge and gad work, there are a number of agate seams in the banks to the north.

Site B is only a few miles farther north, but the road goes through a sandy wash for about 1 mile, making four-wheel drive highly desirable. The tracks follow the wash around the mountain and then continue into a box canyon. From the road's end, search the foothills and washes for opal, green jasper, agate and chalcedony. This locale is not as productive as the others, but is still worth a visit.

The dumps at Site C contain copper ores, including malachite, cuprite, bornite and chrysocolla, as well as some calcite and hematite. These mines have been abandoned for years, but if that no longer appears to be the case, do not trespass!

Looking for Specimens

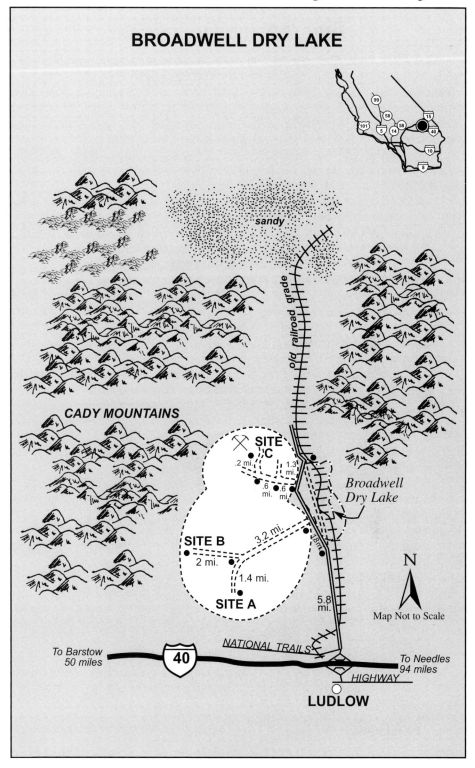

BROADWELL DRY LAKE

sandy

old railroad grade

CADY MOUNTAINS

SITE C

.2 mi.

1.3 mi.

.6 mi.

.6 mi.

Broadwell Dry Lake

SITE B

3.2 mi.

.8 mi.

2 mi.

1.4 mi.

SITE A

5.8 mi.

N

Map Not to Scale

To Barstow
50 miles

40

NATIONAL TRAILS

To Needles
94 miles

HIGHWAY

LUDLOW

99

58

101

5

14

58

15

40

10

8

TUMBLE POLISHING ROCKS

Much of the material that can be found while rock collecting can be tumble polished. Tumbling is the form of stone polishing through which a large segment of rockhounds get in to as a gem hobby. It is a relatively easy craft which produces really beautiful gemstones that can be used in an almost endless variety of jewelry and decorator items. Once the "bug" has bitten you, you may well find yourself branching out into other types of gem cutting and jewelry making. Whatever route you follow, you can be assured you are going to spend many enjoyable, relaxing hours, and you will be able to turn out creations of striking beauty for personal use, gifts, and/or a profitable part-time business.

The following equipment and supplies are needed to become involved in the craft of gemstone tumbling:

(1) **Equipment.** Appropriately, the machine that is used is called a *tumbler*. There is a wide variety of tumblers available, and prices range from quite low to medium, for the most part.

(2) **Rough Gemstone Material.** Many various types of stones are tumble polished, some of the better-known being petrified wood, agate and jade. Craftsmen in this field collect much of the material they use in the deserts, mountains, and in many other locations. The other major source for stones, especially those not available in local areas, is a rock shop or catalog supplier. There you will find rough and polished gemstones; supplies and tools; equipment for all kinds of gem cutting; and mineral and crystal specimens.

(3) **Abrasive (Grit).** *Silicon carbide*, a man-made abrasive in a loose grain or powder form that is used for grinding and smoothing the stones in a tumbler.

(4) **A Polishing Agent.** The final finish is most often accomplished with a polishing powder, usually an oxide of some metal. *Grit* and polishing agents are also sold by rock shops and catalog suppliers.

All of these items may be purchased separately, or some manufacturers do combine them in kit form. In addition to the equipment and materials listed above, these kits usually include a supply of jewelry parts, a tube of jewelry cement and an instruction book. It's a convenient and inexpensive means for getting started in the craft.

There is a wide variety of gem materials available, many of which looks beautiful when tumble polished. They come from three sources:

(1) **Natural minerals formed in the earth.** A few examples of this category include agate, turquoise, garnet, petrified wood and malachite.

(2) **Products of animal or plant life**, such as pearls, coral or amber.

(3) **Man-made materials.** These include synthetics, which are laboratory duplicates of nature, such as synthetic rubies and sapphires.

Of the three categories above, the people who tumble gems use mostly material from the first, the natural stones.

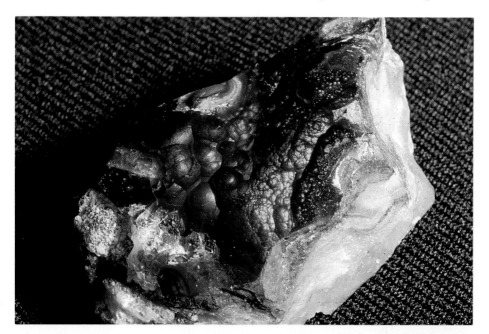

Fire Agate Found Near Palo Verde at the Pebble Terrace Collecting Area

Agate Collected at Afton Canyon Takes a Nice Polish

Geodes and Nodules Collected
at the Hauser Beds

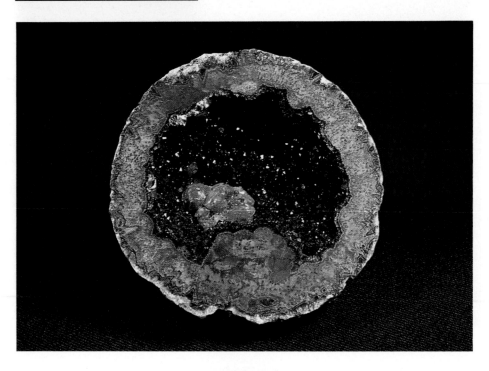

Jasper Found Along Field Road

Jasper and Jasp-Agate Specimens from the Mojave Desert

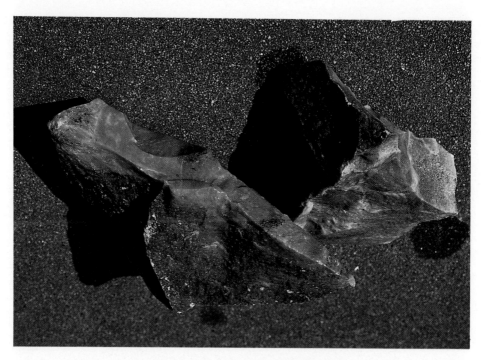

Common Opal From Opal Mountain

Precious Opal Collected in the El Paso Mountains

Pyrolusitic Dendrites Discovered Near the Toltec Mine

Chalcedony Slab From Bedrock Spring

*Shark Teeth From the
Ant Hill Collecting Area*

*Chalcedony Gathered in
the Turtle Mountain*

*Petrified Wood From
the Mojave Desert*

Trona Onyx

Realgar and Orpiment Picked Up in the Danby Collecting Area

Moss Opalite Specimen from Danby

Ulexite Specimens Collected in the Calico Mountains

Iceland Spar (Calcite) Found in the Cady Mountain

TUMBLE POLISHING ROCKS (CONTINUED)

There are many other ways of classifying gemstones. One is the amount of light that can penetrate the material. Thus we have: transparent, semi-transparent, translucent and opaque. All are used for tumble polished gems, but you will probably see more opaque and translucent.

Another classification is by hardness, which in the mineral field is thought of as the ability of one stone to scratch another. This is quite important to the rockhound because generally (not always), the harder the gemstones, the more time required to work it, and the higher polish it will take. Also, the harder the stone, the longer it should retain its polish for there will be fewer substances in its environment that can scratch it.

Friedrich Mohs (1773-1839), a mineralogist, devised a scale for showing hardness with numerical designations of 1 for the softest through 10 for the hardest.

The Mohs Scale of Hardness

1 —	Talc	6 —	Feldspar
2 —	Gypsum	7 —	Quartz
3 —	Calcite	8 —	Topaz
4 —	Fluorite	9 —	Corundum
5 —	Apatite	10 —	Diamond

It should be stated that these are relative hardnesses only. The Mohs Scale simply states that the stones listed will scratch any of those with lower numbers.

It is generally recommended that no material softer than glass be tumbled because they can be scratched easily, ruining the polish. In fact, it is a good idea not to use anything softer than quartz for items that can receive rough treatment—on a key chain, for instance. It is better to use softer stones for earrings, pendants, etc. Exceptions to this rule are the two types of jade, jadeite and nephrite. Although softer than quartz, they do not scratch easily.

For people who collect their own materials in the field, quite a few rock shops and catalog suppliers sell hardness testing kits. These consist of various minerals listed on the Mohs Scale. Inexpensive kits simply have samples of the minerals. On the better sets, pieces of the minerals are mounted in pencil-like handles for easier use.

Tumble polishing is man's improvement on a process that nature has been carrying out for ages. Tons of gemstones are tumbled commercially and sold at reasonable prices. But if you are a do-it-yourselfer, you can save money and have fun tumble polishing your own gems.

From *How to Tumble Polish Gemstones and Make Tumbled Jewelry* by Jerome Wexler.

LAVIC JASPER

Many rockhounds feel that the jasper and jasp-agate from the region surrounding Lavic Road, midway between Ludlow and Hector, is among the best and most colorful to be found in the entire Mojave Desert. Because of that "fame," however, collectors have been converging upon the spot for decades and have severely depleted supplies of the very finest it has to offer. Don't let that deter you since there is still plenty of top quality material to be picked up.

There are two primary collecting areas leading into this field of colorful cutting material. One at its western edge and the other at its east, and virtually all the terrain between offers great potential. To get to Site A, take the Hector Exit from Interstate Highway 40 which is about 32 miles east of Barstow. Go south about 0.1 miles to the National Trails Highway and then drive east 2.4 miles to where some very dim tracks can be seen leading off the pavement to the right (south). Follow those tracks about 0.6 miles and park. From where you park, just roam the terrain in any direction. Look for the brightly colored yellow, red and brown cutting material that has made this region so famous amongst rockhounds. Specimens containing all of the colors together can be used to make very nice polished pieces. Site A is easy to get to, and, while in the area, it might prove to be a very worthwhile stop. But Site B, just a short distance farther east, is centered in what is regarded to be the most productive portion of the gem field. To get there, return to the National Trails Highway and go east 7.2 miles to where the pavement makes a sharp turn to the left (north) onto a bridge crossing the interstate. At that point, Lavic Road leaves the pavement and heads south in the opposite direction. Follow Lavic Road 1.5 miles, as shown on the map, to the center of the collecting area which is only a short distance south of the Lavic Railroad Siding. As was the case at Site A, the quality tends to vary considerably. Take some time to carefully examine what you pick up, and keep only the best.

The jasper and jasp-agate occur in an amazing variety of colors and combinations, primarily tending toward red hues, with blue and white quartz stringers running throughout. Such specimens, especially if they also contain areas of bright yellow and/or orange, make spectacular polished pieces. There is so much to be found at Lavic that you should take the time to carefully sort out all but the very best. Most of the material near the road is somewhat small but larger chunks can be found by doing a little walking.

These two sites, and just about anywhere else nearby, offer countless rockhounding opportunities. The farther from the roads you hike, the better your chances of finding bigger and better specimens. Just don't wander so far from where you park as to lose your bearings.

Site A

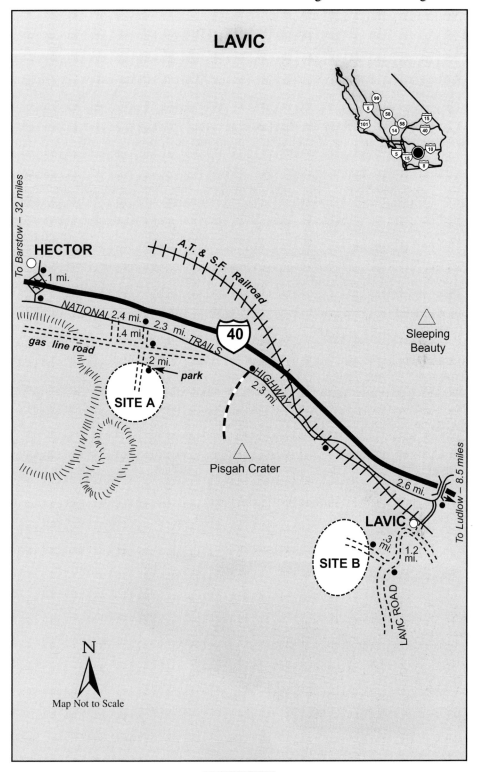

LAVIC

To Barstow – 32 miles

HECTOR

A.T. & S.F. Railroad

1 mi.

NATIONAL 2.4 mi. 2.3 mi. TRAILS

.4 mi.

gas line road

.2 mi.

park

40

Sleeping
Beauty

HIGHWAY
2.3 mi.

SITE A

Pisgah Crater

2.6 mi.

To Ludlow – 8.5 miles

LAVIC

.3 mi.

1.2 mi.

SITE B

LAVIC ROAD

N

Map Not to Scale

HECTOR HILLS

This site has been well-known for many years. Due to its notoriety, most of the surface material, especially near the road, has been taken. Due to the scarcity of what can be found, this should be used as a supplement to a collecting trip, not as a primary destination. The only reason it is mentioned is because there still is some extremely nice agate, jasper, jasp-agate, chalcedony and opalite to be found. It does seems, after each rain, something new is exposed. If you are willing to do some hiking, your chances of finding better quantities increases greatly.

To get to the primary collecting site, take the Hector offramp from Interstate Highway 40, which is about 32 miles east of Barstow. Go south and then east on the National Trails Highway 0.4 miles to where a dirt road intersects on the right. Follow that road just under 0.5 miles and then go right 0.8 miles on the pipeline road and the center of the collecting area. It should be noted that good material can be found all along most of the roads throughout this region and it can often be well worth the time and effort to do some exploration on your own. Drive for a short distance, stop and then sample what can be found. If you have no luck, go a little farther, or take another road and try again.

At the Hector site, material can be found throughout the little hills, primarily south of the road, as illustrated on the accompanying map. The site is extensive, but don't be tempted to do any off-roading. The little hills are composed of loose sand, and even four-wheel drive vehicles can easily get stuck. This is a location which should be explored on foot. The light color of the sandy hills make collecting a little difficult, since much of what can be found occurs in lighter shades, especially the prized agate and chalcedony. One consolation, is that just about any rock you encounter will be something of interest. The jasper, jasp-agate and opalite tends to be yellow, red, purple and orange, thereby being much easier to spot.

Using a sturdy rake to turn the soil is sometimes productive, since it helps uncover otherwise hidden stones. This is a site where patience is required, but what can be found is usually of high quality rewarding the collector who has the perseverance to make the effort.

Looking for Material Along the Road

HECTOR HILLS

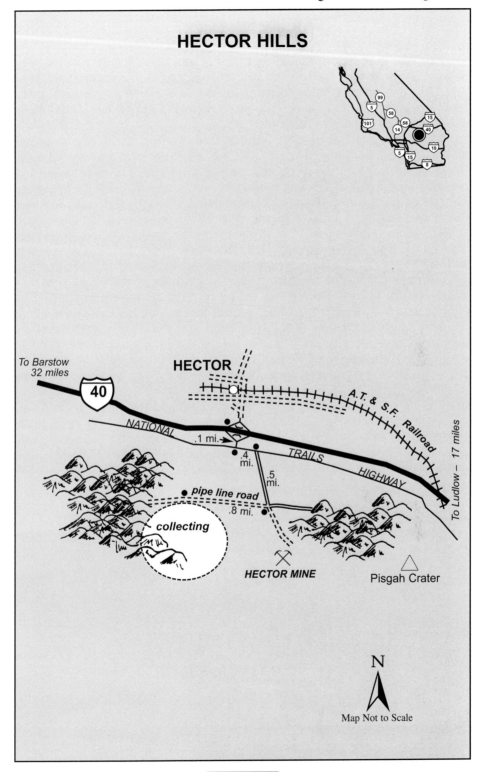

To Barstow
32 miles

40

NATIONAL

HECTOR

A.T. & S.F. Railroad

.1 mi.

.4 mi.

.5 mi.

TRAILS

HIGHWAY

To Ludlow – 17 miles

pipe line road

.8 mi.

collecting

HECTOR MINE

Pisgah Crater

N

Map Not to Scale

JASPER HILL

This site is centered around a small hill which is literally covered with colorful jasper. In fact, the concentration is so high that the orange hue can be detected from nearly a half-mile away. A hike is involved to get there, but a lot of fine material can be picked up near where you must park, if walking is not appealing.

To get to Jasper Hill, go 32 miles east from Barstow to the Hector turnoff and head north. Continue 0.4 miles and bear left at the fork, another 0.8 miles to the railroad tracks. Turn left and parallel the tracks 2.2 more miles to a crossing. This final stretch is very sandy, and four-wheel drive may be necessary.

The crossing gate is usually locked, making it necessary to park and hike the approximately 0.5 miles to the primary collecting site. As mentioned earlier, Jasper Hill is fairly easy to spot, due to its somewhat orange appearance. Simply park south of the tracks and start walking. The jasper is generally found in shades of yellow and orange with black, brown, red and white stringers, some of which is extremely colorful.

If you don't feel like hiking, a lot of very nice material, including chalcedony, agate and, of course, colorful jasper can be found just about anywhere north of the tracks. In fact, the terrain surrounding Jasper Hill offers a better assortment of collectibles then the hill itself. The chalcedony occurs in many hues, including a prize, dark blue variety. The agate also boasts many different colors and patterns, including clear, brown, black and red with some containing showy moss-like inclusions.

It is suggested that you carry some water along, since this is an arid part of the desert. It is also strongly recommended that you DO NOT attempt the trek during the scorching summer months, since temperatures can soar to well above 100° F, and the rocks are often literally too hot to handle. Save this, and most desert locations, for the cooler weather.

The Quarry Near Jasper Hill. A Good Place to Camp or Park When Hiking in.

JASPER HILL

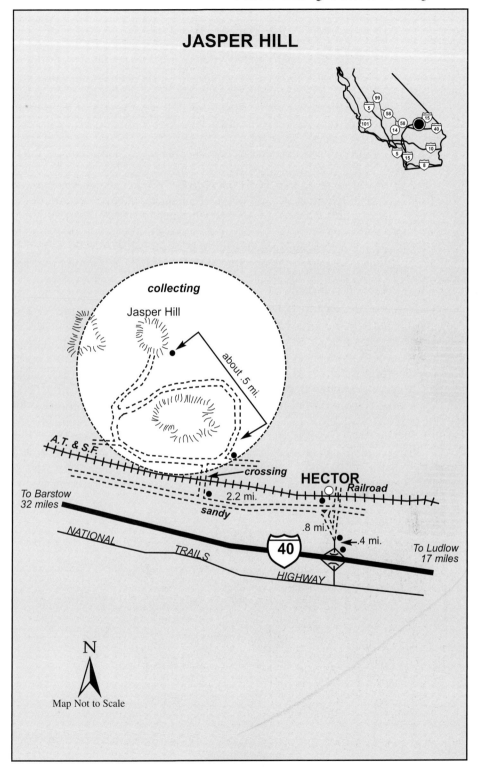

collecting

Jasper Hill

about .5 mi.

A.T. & S.F.

crossing

HECTOR

Railroad

To Barstow
32 miles

2.2 mi.

sandy

.8 mi.

.4 mi.

NATIONAL

TRAILS

40

HIGHWAY

To Ludlow
17 miles

N

Map Not to Scale

NEWBERRY NODULES AND AGATE

Not long ago collectors could gather hundreds of agate-filled nodules in only a few short hours at this location. Today, the little orbs are considerably more difficult to obtain. It is important to note that the center of the nodule site lies right on the northern border of the newly-formed Newberry Mountains Wilderness Area. For this reason, you must hike from the boundary marker a few hundred yards to begin your collecting. The wilderness presents no great inconvenience, since that last stretch of road has been so severely washed out in recent years that a hike was necessary anyway.

To get to this interesting location, take either of the two Newberry Springs exits from Interstate Highway 40 and follow the mileage illustrated on the map to Newberry Road. If traveling from the east, the eastern exit is about 26 miles west of Ludlow. If coming from the west, the western exit is about 19 miles east of Barstow. Upon reaching Newberry Road, go south 0.5 miles to where the pavement ends. At that point, the road gets steep and a little rough. There is an old gate lying beside the road a few tenths of a mile farther along. The gate, a few years ago was locked shut due to some mining activity. That seems to have changed now, but if there is any doubt when you visit, return to the National Trails Highway and check for updated information at the post office.

From the pavement's end, rugged trucks and four-wheel drive units can probably make it the next 0.8 miles to the old quarry, where you should park. The nodules and occasional geodes were formed within the crumbly white regions above the wash, which can easily be seen from the road leading into the mountains. Hike into the canyon, paying particular attention to those light regions or look through the rubble immediately below. Most specimens tend to be quite small, but some have been found measuring more than 5 inches across. A respectable percentage contain agate or crystal centers but there are quite a few duds. It takes some hard work and exploration to find a worthwhile quantity, but that effort is usually rewarded with fine specimens.

NEWBERRY

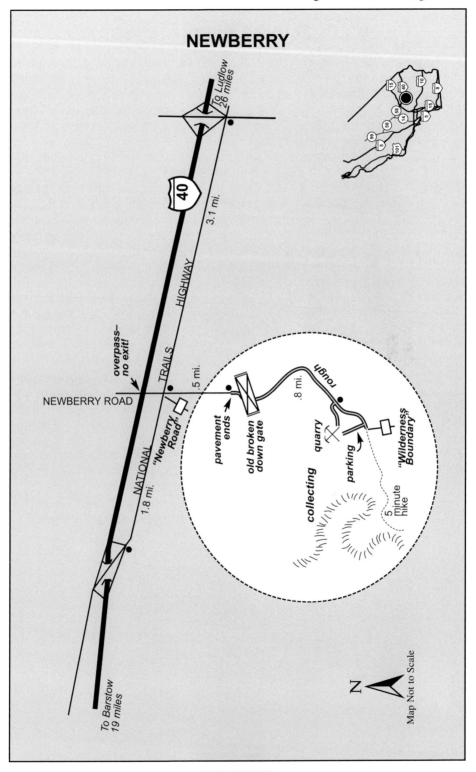

To Ludlow
26 miles

40

3.1 mi.

HIGHWAY

overpass—
no exit!

TRAILS

.5 mi.

NEWBERRY ROAD

"Newberry
Road"

NATIONAL

1.8 mi.

pavement
ends

old broken
down gate

rough

.8 mi.

quarry

collecting

parking

5 minute
hike

"Wilderness
Boundary"

To Barstow
19 miles

N

Map Not to Scale

ORD MOUNTAIN

Just below the abandoned Grandview Gold Mine situated on Ord Mountain, overlooking Lucerne Valley, one can collect unusual orbicular rhyolite. It is found scattered all over the slopes and occurs in a wide range of colors and patterns. To get to this interesting and productive collecting location, take State Highway 247 for 4.8 miles east from where it intersected State Highway 18 in town. At that point, turn to the north onto Camp Rock Road and go 3.7 miles, bear right, staying on Camp Rock Road, and continue another 9 miles onto the slopes of Ord Mountain. All but the last 7 miles is paved, and the road is well-graded on the gravel portions. Most rugged vehicles can make this trip, and even a passenger car should have no trouble, if driven cautiously.

Park anywhere near the given mileage and search the hillsides for the spotted rhyolite, most of which is filled with little "eyes." There is a lot to be found, but some is considerably better than other. Take the time to find material with the most pronounced "eyes" and minimal pitting. A lot of the rhyolite is porous and won't take a polish, so pay attention to what you pick up. You can either drive or walk for quite a distance along the slopes. Keep in mind that this has long been a popular collecting location, so regions nearest to the main road have been heavily picked over. For that reason, short walks might prove to be fruitful.

Most of the "eyes" are perfectly round, with some measuring up to 0.25 inches in diameter. On some specimens, they are very distorted and produce fascinating display pieces. This material is not only fun to collect, but it is equally enjoyable to cut and polish. How you orient the saw will help determine how the "eyes" will look. Perfectly round, tear drop, oblique or just plain distorted "eyes" are all possibilities. This material is best used for larger pieces, since the final polish is generally not high gloss. It is great for bookends, clock faces and, occasionally, cabochons.

About 1 mile farther up the mountain, as illustrated on the map, is the Grandview Mine. More of the orbicular rhyolite can be found there, as well as a spectacular view of Lucerne Valley and the distant San Bernardino Mountains. The dumps are flat, and it is possible to camp there, if you want to spend some time. It often gets quite windy, but the spectacular view and the solitude can make it a memorable place to spend an evening.

ORD MOUNTAIN

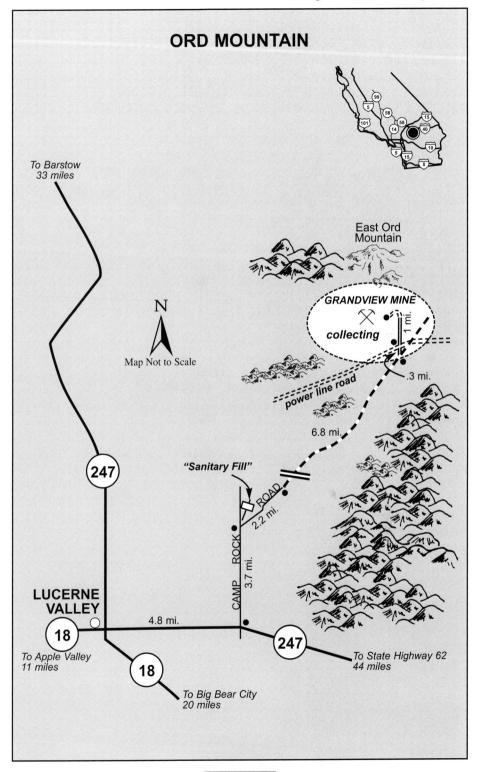

East Ord
Mountain

GRANDVIEW MINE

collecting

1 mi.

power line road

.3 mi.

6.8 mi.

N

Map Not to Scale

247

"Sanitary Fill"

ROAD

2.2 mi.

CAMP ROCK

3.7 mi.

LUCERNE
VALLEY

18

4.8 mi.

247

To Barstow
33 miles

To Apple Valley
11 miles

18

To Big Bear City
20 miles

To State Highway 62
44 miles

STODDARD WELL

The Rodman Mountains, just a short distance north of Victorville, provide the rockhound with very colorful marble. To get to the first of the three sites illustrated on the accompanying map, go north on Interstate Highway 15 from Victorville 3.8 miles from the "E" Street turnoff (State Highway 18 to Apple Valley). At that point, take the Stoddard Wells Road offramp and proceed 9.7 miles. The pavement ends after having gone 4.2 miles, but the gravel road is well maintained and most rugged vehicles should have no problem.

When you reach the given mileage, bear right off the main road and drive another 1.2 miles to the base of the mountain and park. Hike to the mine which can be seen high on the mountain. Do not be tempted to drive all the way to the quarry. The old road leading up is severely washed out in places, extremely steep and very dangerous. The hike is not easy, but if you take your time and carry some water, it isn't bad. Do not attempt the trek if you have any doubts about your physical condition. Sites B and C are far more accessible.

Site A boasts a beautiful, brilliant and yellow-green marble and it is generally very solid, capable of producing nice polished pieces. It is known locally as Verde Antique Marble, and is worth the effort to obtain. Most of the prime surface chips and stones have been picked up long ago, so it is necessary to use hard rock tools, such as gads, chisels, sledgehammers, pry bars, gloves and goggles to directly remove the best from its place in the quarry walls. Quality varies considerably here. Try to get that with the most saturated color as possible.

To get to Site B, return to the main road, go 0.9 miles, and then turn right going another 0.6 miles to the small dump. There you will be able to get more of the Verde Antique Marble, but quality and size of the deposit are not nearly as good as at Site A. The final few tenths of a mile are a little rough, so you may have to park and hike the remaining distance.

Site C is known for its beautiful tri-colored marble. To get there, take Stoddard Well Road another 1.3 miles, go right on the Lucerne Valley Road 3.9 miles, and then right again, proceeding 2.2 miles to yet another quarry. The last 2 miles is fairly rutted, but most rugged, high clearance vehicles should be able to make it all the way. Site C boasts marble in a variety of colors, including pink, green, white, brown and black. Some marble pieces are very nice, especially if it contains saturated hues of pink, green and white, all together. As was the case before, the best material must be obtained directly from the deposit and the quality varies considerably.

Hiking at Site A

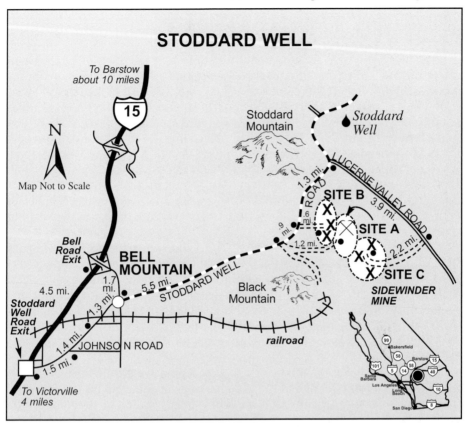

STODDARD WELL

To Barstow
about 10 miles

15

N

Map Not to Scale

Stoddard
Mountain

*Stoddard
Well*

1.3 mi.

LUCERNE VALLEY ROAD

ROAD

SITE B

3.9 mi.

.6 mi.

.9 mi.

SITE A

1.2 mi.

2.2 mi.

Bell
Road
Exit

**BELL
MOUNTAIN**

1.7
mi.

5.5 mi.

STODDARD WELL

SITE C

SIDEWINDER
MINE

4.5 mi.

1.3 mi.

Black
Mountain

**Stoddard
Well
Road
Exit**

1.4 mi.

JOHNSON ROAD

railroad

1.5 mi.

To Victorville
4 miles

99
Bakersfield
58
58 Barstow 15
101 5 14 58
Santa
Barbara
Los Angeles 40
Long
Beach 10
San Diego 8

Carrying Specimens Back to the Truck at Site C

SAN GABRIEL MOUNTAINS ACTINOLITE

Much of the region west and southwest of the small town of Wrightwood offers mineral collectors an opportunity to gather good specimens of fibrous green actinolite. To get there, take the State Highway 138 Exit from Interstate Highway 15, which is about 21 miles north of San Bernardino and 20 miles south of Victorville. Follow State Highway 138 west 8.5 miles to where you must turn left onto State Highway 2, proceeding 4.7 miles to Wrightwood. From Wrightwood, drive another 4.7 miles on State Highway 2 and then, instead of continuing straight onto Road N4, go left, staying on State Highway 2. From that last turn, potential collecting can be accessed anywhere from 5 to 7 miles farther. Pull off the pavement at a safe spot, and explore areas of erosion. Look primarily in washes and streambeds for chunks of the soft but nice and unusual collectible.

The two most important things to keep in mind when at this site is to park in a safe place off the pavement and to park somewhere where you have easy access to a wash or little canyon within which to conduct your search. Since State Highway 2 winds its way through this mountainous region, accomplishing both tasks is not as easy as it might sound. There are also a lot of trees in the area, further complicating the quest for the perfect place to stop. With all of that in mind, it is still a nice locale, especially during the summer spring and fall.

If you don't have much luck at one spot, just drive a little farther and try again. After you have explored the terrain alongside State Highway 2, it might be fruitful to take any side road leading off the pavement that you might encounter all the way back to Wrightwood. Be advised that most of the intersecting roads are not paved, so be sure your vehicle can travel on whichever roads you choose. Some are much rougher than others and most are not designed for passenger cars.

Road Passing Through the Site

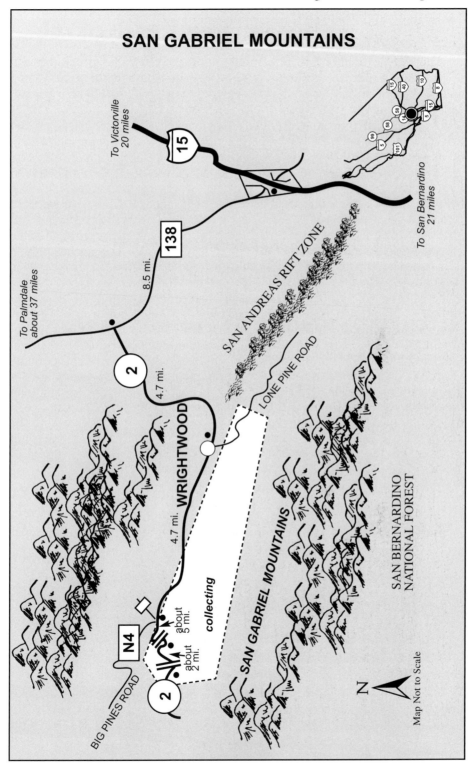

SAN GABRIEL MOUNTAINS

To Victorville
20 miles

15

To Palmdale
about 37 miles

138

8.5 mi.

2

4.7 mi.

WRIGHTWOOD

4.7 mi.

To San Bernardino
21 miles

SAN ANDREAS RIFT ZONE

LONE PINE ROAD

collecting

SAN GABRIEL MOUNTAINS

SAN BERNARDINO
NATIONAL FOREST

N4

2

BIG PINES ROAD

about
5 mi.

about
2 mi.

N

Map Not to Scale

NEWHALL FOSSILS

This site lies within the boundaries of the Angeles National Forest but is very close to some large population centers. In spite of the frequent congestion and huge numbers of people in the region, this site is like a little oasis away from it all. Not only is it an oasis, but it is a place where you have a chance to find fossilized leaves from trees that lived here about 12 million years ago. Just to discover a remnant of such an ancient living thing is a fascinating experience. Be advised that it takes patience, care and persistence to find much.

To get this interesting location take State Highway 14 to the Sand Canyon Exit, which is 8.5 miles northeast of where it intersects Interstate Highway 5 near Newhall. Go north on Sand Canyon Road 1.8 miles to Mint Canyon Road, turn right (east), going only 0.7 miles to Vasquez Canyon Road, where you should then turn left (north). From there, the route takes you through some interesting badlands as it leads into the famous fossil-bearing Mint Canyon Formation. Rarely, fossils which include gastropods and pelecypods have been found within the brownish deposits, but most of the area is on private property, thereby limiting most collecting opportunities.

The primary collecting site is accessed by continuing northward 3.6 miles from where you turned onto Vasquez Canyon Road and then going right on Bouquet Canyon Road. Go another 0.7 miles and then north onto Coarse Gold Road, which is dirt but fairly well maintained. Be advised that Bouquet Canyon Road is well traveled and Coarse Gold Road is tough to spot. Maintain an awareness of traffic before slowing to an unreasonable pace or slamming on your brakes. Follow Coarse Gold Road about 1 mile to where there is a good turnout on the right (east) in which to park.

The fossil leaf collecting is done east of the parking area in the brilliant white chalky looking areas which are easily spotted starting about 50 yards down the hill. Be careful as you scramble down to the deposit and again, be reminded that it takes luck and a lot of patience to find much here, but it is a fun place to explore. Carefully examine any chunks of the white volcanic tuff for traces of the elusive leaves. There is sumac, sycamore, live oak and mountain mahogany, to name a few of the different varieties you can find.

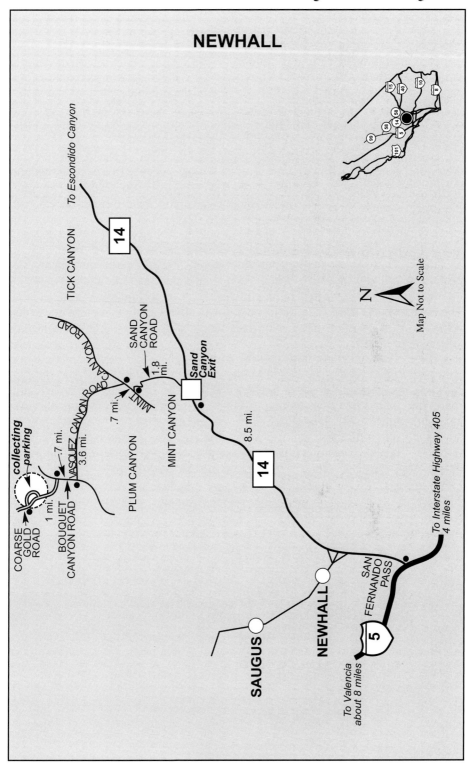

NEWHALL

N

Map Not to Scale

To Escondido Canyon

14

TICK CANYON

CANYON ROAD

SAND CANYON ROAD

1.8 mi.

Sand Canyon Exit

MINT CANYON

.7 mi.

collecting parking

.7 mi.

VASQUEZ CANYON ROAD

3.6 mi.

COARSE GOLD ROAD

BOUQUET CANYON ROAD

1 mi.

PLUM CANYON

8.5 mi.

14

To Interstate Highway 405
4 miles

SAUGUS

NEWHALL

SAN FERNANDO PASS

5

To Valencia
about 8 miles

CASTLE BUTTE

The area surrounding prominent Castle Butte has long been known amongst Southern California rockhounds as a reliable source of jasper, agate, opalite, petrified palm wood, chalcedony and jasp-agate. Most of the roads through here are not bad, and any rugged vehicle shouldn't have a problem if it isn't wet. Just about any place you stop within the boundaries of the accompanying map will provide good collecting potential.

To get to Site A, go north from State Highway 58, at North Edwards on Clay Mine Road, which is about 18 miles east of Mojave. Drive 2.1 miles and then go west 0.5 miles into the hills. Throughout those hills one can find chalcedony and occasional pieces of jasper and agate. All are somewhat scarce, but what is there is usually very nice.

Continue north on Clay Mine Road another 1.4 miles, turn northwest, and stop just about anywhere within the extensive region designated on the map as Site B. There you can find petrified wood, petrified palm, agate, opalite, jasp-agate and jasper. Much of the surface material has long ago been picked up, making it necessary to do some digging in order to find sizable specimens. The best wood is buried up to six feet down, but the labor is often rewarded with beautiful samples. Look for places where others have dug as indicators on where to start.

The easiest and generally most productive collecting in the Castle Butte area is at Site C, which is reached by again going north on Clay Mine Road to Aerial Acres, a small group of trailers and homes. From there, turn left and follow the instructions on the map. This is the primary Castle Butte collecting location, and outstanding material is available everywhere throughout the slopes of the mountain, all the way down to the flatlands. This prolific location offers jasp-agate, chalcedony, jasper, petrified wood, petrified palm, opalite and agate, as well as very nice green bloodstone.

A View of Castle Butte

CASTLE BUTTE

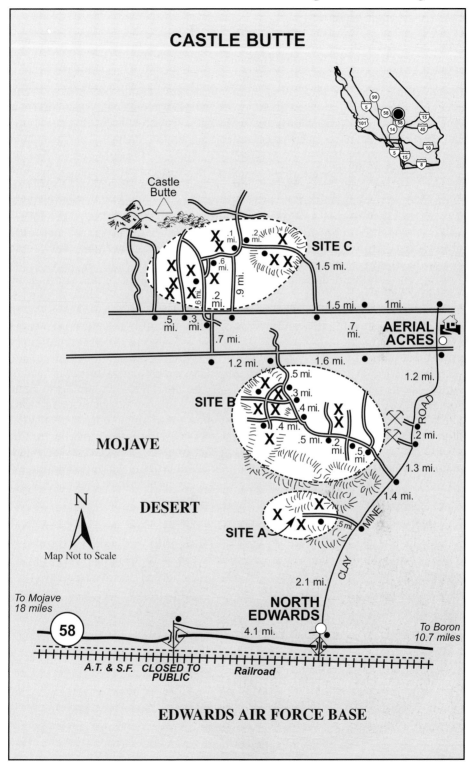

Castle
Butte

SITE C
1.5 mi.

.1 mi.
.2 mi.
.6 mi.
.2 mi.
.9 mi.
.6 mi.

1.5 mi. 1mi.

.5 mi. .3 mi.

.7 mi.

.7 mi.

AERIAL ACRES

1.2 mi. 1.6 mi.

1.2 mi.

.5 mi.
.3 mi.
.4 mi.
.4 mi.
.5 mi. .2 mi. .5 mi.

SITE B

MOJAVE

.2 mi.

1.3 mi.

1.4 mi.

DESERT

N

Map Not to Scale

SITE A
.5 mi.

CLAY MINE
ROAD

2.1 mi.

To Mojave
18 miles

58

NORTH EDWARDS
4.1 mi.

To Boron
10.7 miles

A.T. & S.F. **CLOSED TO PUBLIC** *Railroad*

EDWARDS AIR FORCE BASE

NORTH EDWARDS ONYX

Colorful, banded travertine onyx can be obtained just a short distance from the town of North Edwards. For many years this has been an active claim owned by the Sierra Pelona Rock Club, (write to them at P.O. Box 221256, Newhall, CA 91322, e-mail them at rhyde83@earthlink.net, or visit their website at http://home.earthlink.net/~rhyde83/) and rockhounds are allowed to collect there, as long as they register. The club simply wants to know how many people go there and how long they work, so the information can be applied toward fulfilling their annual assessment work requirement.

To get to this most productive spot, take the Clay Mine Road Exit from State Highway 58 at North Edwards. Proceed north 6.2 miles to Aerial Acres, a small group of homes and trailers, and turn right. Continue 2 more miles, and then go left onto the dim ruts another 0.3 miles to the diggings. That final turn comes just as you crest onto a little ridge, making the tracks difficult to see, so be attentive.

The onyx obtained here is very nice, but it takes a lot of work to get the best. You will need gads, chisels, a sledgehammer, pry bars, gloves, goggles and a lot of energy if you decide to directly attack any of the deposits. If you don't feel like engaging in strenuous sledgehammer work, there are many nice specimens scattered throughout the surrounding landscape. The best, definitely must be obtained by directly removing it from the source.

Most of the onyx is beautifully banded, in vivid shades of gold, brown, white, black, red and yellow, with each of the digging pits seeming to offer something a little different. The most ardently sought material is that with alternate red and white banding, but everything else also tends to be of very high quality. Due to the immense diversity of colors and patterns, be sure to inspect as much of the area as you can in order to determine exactly where you want to expend your energy. Most of the local material is very solid and takes a good polish. Exquisite lapidary items can be made from it, including cabochons, clock faces, bookends and spheres.

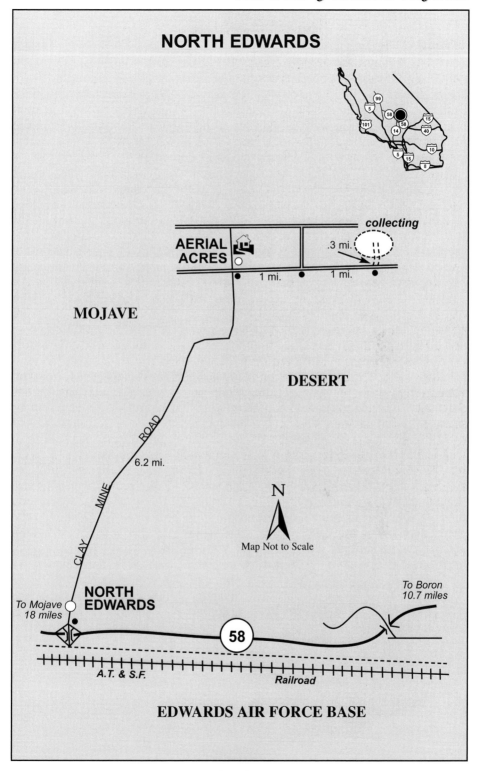

NORTH EDWARDS

collecting

AERIAL ACRES

.3 mi.

1 mi.   1 mi.

MOJAVE

DESERT

ROAD

MINE

CLAY

6.2 mi.

N

Map Not to Scale

NORTH EDWARDS

To Mojave 18 miles

To Boron 10.7 miles

58

A.T. & S.F.   Railroad

EDWARDS AIR FORCE BASE

KRAMER HILLS

The Kramer Hills have long afforded rockhounds many fine collecting possibilities, and in spite of all that has been removed over the years, there still seems to be a lot left. To get there, take U.S. Highway 395 south from Kramer Junction (Four Corners) about 0.4 miles, bear left onto the dirt road another 2.7 miles, turn right, and drive 1.1 more miles to the turnoff to Site A, as illustrated on the map.

At Site A and at nearby Site B, one can find agate and jasper, as well as small quantities of petrified palm, scattered throughout the surrounding terrain. Just park and explore as much of the landscape as you have the time and energy for.

The best-known of the Kramer Hills locations is probably Site C, the Kee Kay Prospect. This, at one time, was a privately owned claim, but permission was granted to anyone wishing to collect there, as long as they notified the owner. That information was needed to fulfill annual assessment work requirements. Current ownership status was unavailable at the time of publication, so you must use good judgment when you are there. If that requirement is still mandated, please follow through. If it appears closed to collecting, which is doubtful, be sure to respect the rights of the claim holders and gather specimens elsewhere in this highly productive area.

Site C offers green autunite; red, brown, moss and flower agate; and petrified palm. The material is found in float, as well as in veins. You can obtain small pieces of gem peridot in the black volcanic ridge east of the diggings. The mounds between that ridge and the primary deposit contain salmon-colored dendritic opal and colorful agate.

Throughout the valley south of Site C is more agate, jasper, petrified palm and opalite. This general location is designated as Site D on the map.

Our final Kramer Hills location, Site E, is reached by returning to U.S. Highway 395 and driving south 5.6 miles. At that point, turn east onto the ruts and go around the little hill 0.4 miles. In the wash, near where you must park, scant amounts of colorful chalcedony and agate can be found. The prime spot is on the overlooking ridge. Hike into the saddle and search throughout the soft soil surrounding the little sink hole. There, you can gather beautiful jasper, agate and some very nice onyx. Be sure to fully explore as much of this region as possible, since material can be found throughout the area.

*Searching for
Specimens
in the Site E*

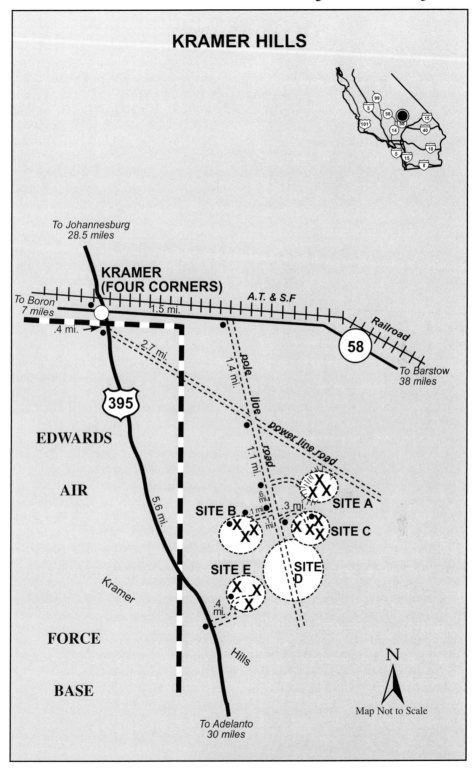

KRAMER HILLS

To Johannesburg
28.5 miles

**KRAMER
(FOUR CORNERS)**

A.T. & S.F

1.5 mi.

To Boron
7 miles

.4 mi.

2.7 mi.

Railroad

58

To Barstow
38 miles

395

EDWARDS

AIR

pole line road

1.4 mi.

power line road

1.1 mi.

5.6 mi.

.6 mi.

SITE A
X X

SITE B
X X

.1 mi.

.3 mi.

SITE C
X X X

.1 mi.

SITE E
X X
X

SITE D

.4 mi.

Kramer

Hills

FORCE

BASE

N

Map Not to Scale

To Adelanto
30 miles

OPAL MOUNTAIN

Opal Mountain is just what the name implies, a mountain crisscrossed with seams of beautiful opal, some of which is filled with fire. Be advised, though, that most of what can be found is common opal, void of fire, but it does occur in an amazing variety of vivid colors. The hues seem limitless, but most is in shades of honey, green, orange, red, yellow and white. In addition, some of the sites lie within the newly formed Black Mountain Wilderness. Familiarize yourself with regulations governing those areas and remember that vehicles are not allowed beyond the wilderness boundary markers.

In the early 1900s, Scouts Cove produced precious opal, as well as some beautiful cherry and orange common opal. The best seams were approximately 200 feet below the surface and encased within very hard rock. Due to the extreme expense involved in removing the spectacular gemstones, the operation was forced to close. Occasionally, a lucky rockhound will stumble upon a small specimen of that amazing material, but it generally is no more than a small chip.

To get to Opal Mountain, take Hinkley Road north from State Highway 58, which is about 15 miles west of Barstow. Go 7.5 miles, bear right at the fork, drive another 3.9 miles, and proceed left 5.6 more miles to the turn to the first of many Opal Mountain collecting spots. From that point, use the map as an approximate guide to only some of the numerous other high potential rockhounding locations. Once in the general region depicted on the map, just about any place you stop offers potential for finding not only common opal but also some very colorful agate and jasper. Just park randomly and do some walking. If you don't find much at the first stop, drive a little farther and try again.

What seems to be the most productive of the Opal Mountain sites are shown on the map, and you should definitely try to visit as many of those as possible. Most of the opal occurs in seams and, therefore, must be removed from the encasing rock with heavy tools, such as sledgehammers, gads and chisels. There are generally some small pieces lying around, but if you want the best, it is necessary to attack the deposits themselves. Be sure to wear gloves and goggles if you do decide to work the seams, since, when struck, the glass-like opal often shatters, sending needle-like splinters rocketing through the air.

Working the seams is DIFFICULT work, but if you have the energy and determination, you may be able to extract some exquisite specimens. In order to get worthwhile pieces, it is essential that you first carefully break down the tough surrounding rock before trying to remove any opal. Otherwise, all you will have is a colorful collection of opal splinters.

OPAL MOUNTAIN

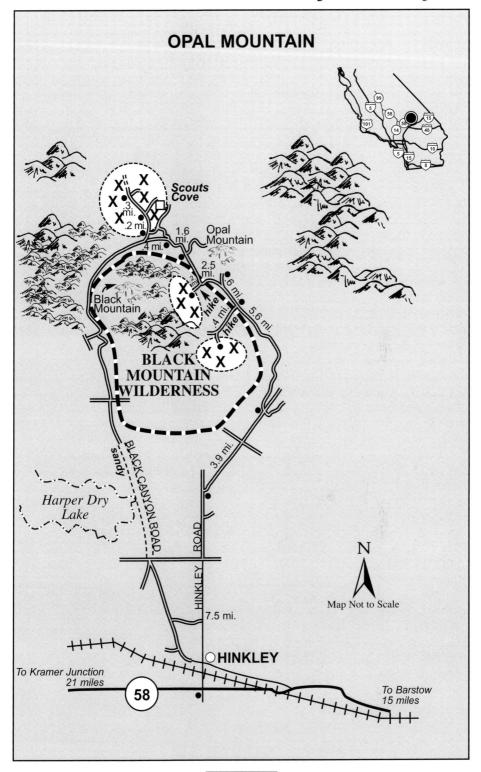

Scouts Cove

.3 mi.

.2 mi.

1.6 mi.

.4 mi.

Opal Mountain

2.5 mi.

.2 mi.

.6 mi.

5.6 mi.

.4 mi.

hike

hike

Black Mountain

BLACK MOUNTAIN WILDERNESS

BLACK CANYON ROAD

sandy

Harper Dry Lake

3.9 mi.

HINKLEY   ROAD

7.5 mi.

N

Map Not to Scale

⊙**HINKLEY**

To Kramer Junction
21 miles

58

To Barstow
15 miles

COYOTE DRY LAKE

Bright, white onyx can be found on the dumps of an old quarry, about 17 miles north of Barstow. To get there, take Fort Irwin Road north from town 5.4 miles to the turnoff to Rainbow Basin. If you have time, this is a geological and paleontological wonderland. It is filled with fascinating and colorful formations and an incredible variety of fossils, including bones from saber-tooth tigers. NO COLLECTING of any kind is allowed within the boundaries of Rainbow Basin, but it does feature a nice campground and is a fascinating place to see.

To get to the onyx, continue north toward Fort Irwin another 12.3 miles, turn right onto the dirt road, and drive another 2.2 miles. At the given mileage, some ruts head off to the right toward the mountains and the easily seen diggings, those being the onyx mine dumps and the center of the collecting area. As is the case with all abandoned mines, if it appears that this one is no longer deserted or that collecting is no longer allowed, do not trespass.

Most of the local onyx is solid white, but some have delicate bands of black and gray. Occasionally, there are cavities which are filled with tiny calcite crystals. It often takes some splitting with chisels and a sledgehammer to expose the crystal pockets, but just finding a few such specimens should make the effort worthwhile.

Collectors can also find small garnet crystals and massive green epidote throughout the dumps, usually in combination with the onyx. A specimen of the bright, white onyx covered with deep red garnets, in association with green epidote and/or crystal pockets is outstanding for display. It takes time to find the best, but once you find a few chunks of the good material, subsequent pieces are easier to locate.

Examining a Rock at Coyote Dry Lake

COYOTE DRY LAKE

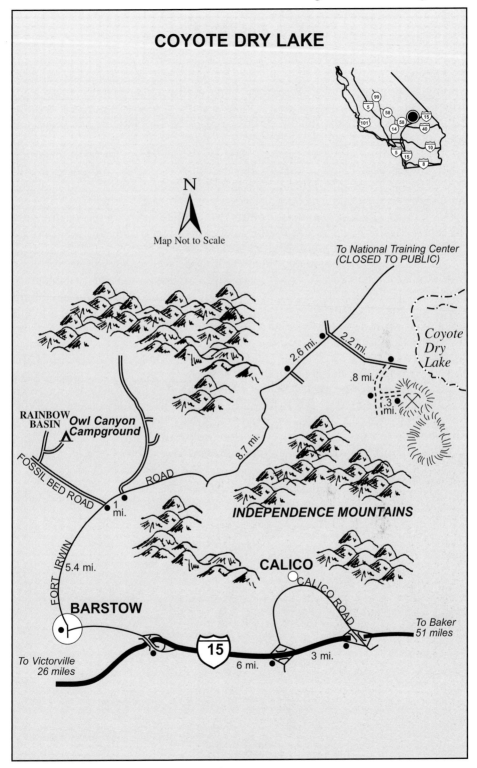

N

Map Not to Scale

To National Training Center
(CLOSED TO PUBLIC)

Coyote Dry Lake

2.6 mi.   2.2 mi.

.8 mi.

.3 mi.

RAINBOW BASIN
Owl Canyon Campground

FOSSIL BED ROAD

ROAD

8.7 mi.

1 mi.

INDEPENDENCE MOUNTAINS

FORT IRWIN

5.4 mi.

CALICO

CALICO ROAD

BARSTOW

To Baker
51 miles

15

To Victorville
26 miles

6 mi.   3 mi.

CALICO MOUNTAINS

The scenic Calico Mountains have long been a favorite location for rockhounds to pursue their hobby. The supply seems to be limitless and the variety astounding. Be advised that some of the roads are becoming very rough and washed out, making it necessary to hike a short distance. Four-wheel drive is probably not necessary, but be sure to use good judgment and don't take your vehicle anywhere it is not designed to go.

To get to the Calico Mountains, take the Calico Road Exit from Interstate Highway 15, which is about 10.8 miles east of Barstow. From there, go north 0.8 miles and then turn right onto Mule Canyon Road. From there, follow the map to get to the various collecting areas.

Site A is situated about 0.1 miles up a steep road, and it is probably advisable to park below and walk up. A lot of jasp-agate can be found for quite a distance in all directions. Site B boasts agate, sagenite and chalcedony throughout the overlooking cliffs. The chalcedony occurs in a variety of colors, and is found on boulders littering the hillside. Easily spotted excavations mark places where veins of agate and sagenite can be found, and if you have hard rock tools such as a sledgehammer, gads, chisels, gloves and goggles, it might be worth your time to attack some of those seams.

Site C features small amounts of chalcedony and jasper, with the most highly-prized being a beautiful goldenlace variety. Inspect both sides of the road, as well as the diggings to the north.

The last spot, Site D, is noted for its plentiful supply of agate, petrified palm and petrified wood. All is found in float, on both sides of the road, for quite a distance. Just park anywhere along this stretch and explore the surrounding terrain. As is the case with most rockhounding sites, the farther from the main road you get, the more you usually find.

CALICO MOUNTAINS

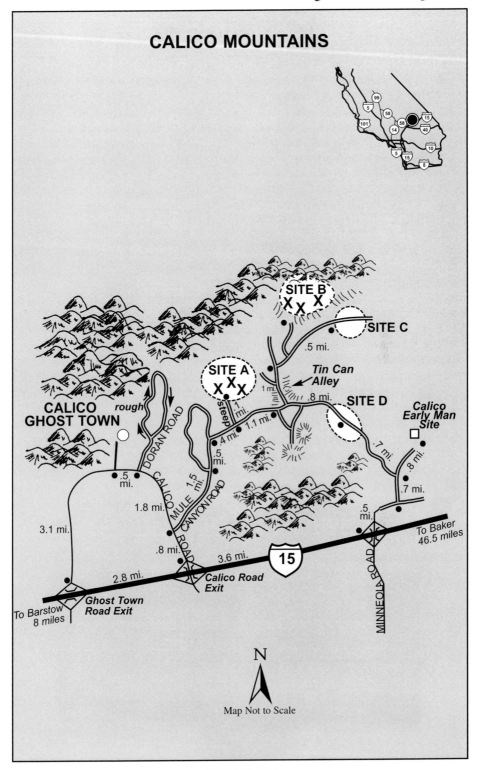

SITE B
X X X

SITE C

.5 mi.

SITE A
X X X

Tin Can
Alley

1 mi.

.8 mi.

SITE D

Calico
Early Man
Site

CALICO
GHOST TOWN

rough

steep

1 mi.

1.1 mi.

.4 mi.

.5
mi.

1.5
mi.

.7 mi.

.8
mi.

DORAN ROAD

CALICO

MULE CANYON ROAD

.5
mi.

1.8 mi.

.7 mi.

3.1 mi.

.8 mi.

.5
mi.

To Baker
46.5 miles

3.6 mi.

15

2.8 mi.

Calico Road
Exit

MINNEOLA ROAD

To Barstow
8 miles

Ghost Town
Road Exit

N

Map Not to Scale

YERMO

Agate, petrified palm root, jasper and chert can be gathered throughout the region surrounding the Calico Early Man Site, a short distance from Barstow. To get to this interesting locality, go east on Interstate Highway 15 for about 13 miles to the Minneola Road Exit. Proceed north a very short distance, and turn right, going another 0.5 miles to Site A. At that point, the collecting commences. All along the road, for at least 0.5 miles, one can find sparse amounts of nice agate and occasional chunks of petrified palm root. This is labeled Site A on the map.

To get to Site B, go back and then north 0.9 miles, instead of proceeding straight ahead. At that point, turn right, as shown on the map, and park anywhere along the old pole line road for at least 0.5 miles. Just walk in any direction, looking for agate and petrified palm.

While in the area, it would be a shame not to visit the Calico Early Man Site, about 0.8 miles northeast of Site B. There you can see the excavations where man-made items dating back approximately 200,000 years have been found. This archaeological site has provided scientists the earliest dated evidence for human occupation in the western hemisphere.

Collecting Site C is accessed by going northwest 0.7 miles from the Calico Early Man turnoff. The somewhat rough road is often difficult to spot. Maintenance tractors regularly clear the route to the Calico Early Man Site, thereby forming quite a sizable berm on the side of the main road. Sometimes the berm is so high that it is virtually impossible for vehicles to get over. It might be advisable to park and walk.

At the given mileage, follow the tracks to the right about 0.1 miles to a good place to camp, and the center of Site C. Site D is only 0.3 miles farther along.

Roam throughout the hills surrounding both locations to find petrified palm, jasper, chert and agate in shades of white, brown and tan. The greenish-colored hills seem to be more productive than other areas.

The Collecting Site C

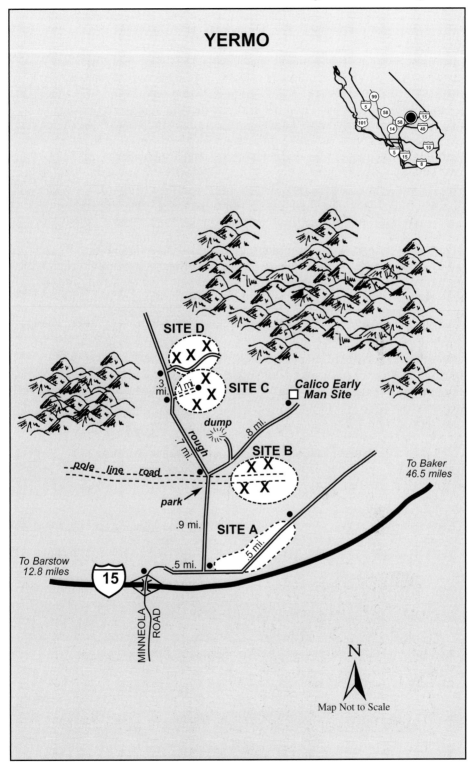

YERMO

SITE D

SITE C

Calico Early Man Site

.3 mi.

.1 mi.

dump

.7 mi.

rough

8 mi.

pole line road

park

SITE B

To Baker 46.5 miles

.9 mi.

SITE A

.5 mi.

.5 mi.

To Barstow 12.8 miles

15

MINNEOLA ROAD

N

Map Not to Scale

AFTON CANYON

Afton Canyon offers one of the most scenic collecting locations in the entire desert. To get to the main canyon, it is necessary to ford the Mojave River. Most of the time, this does not present s problem since the riverbed is primarily rock and gravel, and the water is usually shallow.

To get to Afton Canyon, go east on Interstate Highway 15 about 32 miles from Barstow, or west about 25 miles from Baker to the Afton turnoff. Proceed south, past the campground for 4.7 miles, and then turn right, crossing the riverbed. Just after crossing, turn right, go over the tracks, and follow the ruts into the canyon. It can be very sandy in places, so be careful not to get stuck.

The best collecting is generally within the side canyons and on the upper hills, involving quite a hike from the main canyon floor where you must park. Look for flame, banded, lace and moss agate; sagenite; brown, yellow, red, orange and bloodstone jasper; jasp-agate; and opalite in shades of green and yellow. A lot of bubbly chalcedony can also be found, most of which is white, but some occurs in beautiful pink and purple hues. About halfway through the main canyon you will see a ledge composed of rhombohedral calcite crystals. They are fascinating and great for display in mineral collections.

If you decide to hike into some of the side canyons, be very careful. Not only watch your footing, but also be certain you do not lose your bearings. There has been recent talk of declaring the Afton Canyon area off limits to vehicles. If that is the case, it might be necessary to park near the railroad tracks and hike from there. That should present only minimal hardship, since the walk is very pleasant, the scenery spectacular, and a lot of very good material washes to the lower areas every year.

View of Afton Canyon

AFTON CANYON

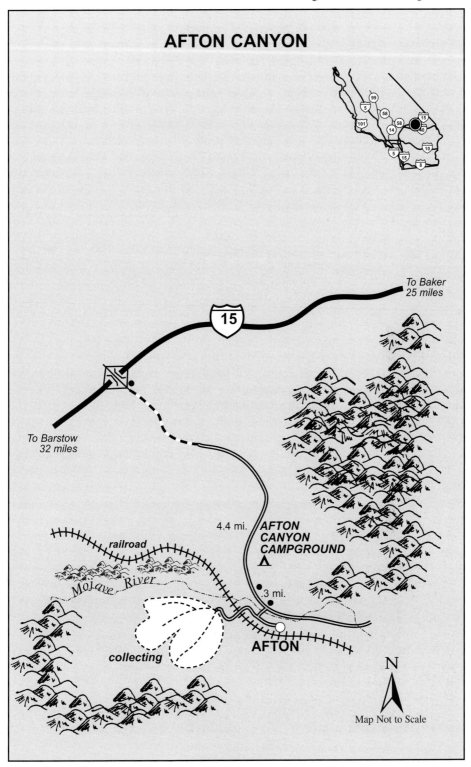

To Baker
25 miles

15

To Barstow
32 miles

4.4 mi. **AFTON CANYON CAMPGROUND**

railroad

Mojave River

.3 mi.

collecting

AFTON

N

Map Not to Scale

ALVORD MOUNTAINS

Good specimens of brightly colored jasper, quality agate, interesting rhombohedral calcite crystals, chrysocolla, malachite and hematite can all be found in and around the site of the now abandoned Alvord Gold Mine. To get there from Interstate Highway 15, take either the Harvard Road turnoff, which is about 23 miles east of Barstow, or the Field Road turnoff, about 33 miles west of Baker. Proceed on the road just south of the interstate 3.2 miles east from Harvard Road or 4.1 miles west from Field Road, and then head north. Be advised that the road to the Alvord Mine, especially as you enter the foothills, gets very rough in places. Use good judgment as to how far you can go. Four-wheel drive probably isn't necessary, but it might be nice.

Drive into the hills 6.1 miles, passing Alvord Well along the way. Then turn right to the Alvord Mine, another rough 0.4 miles. As is the case with any mine site, collecting status may change from time to time. The site has been abandoned for many years, but there is always the possibility it may again be reopened. If there is any indication that collecting is no longer allowed, do not trespass. Restrict your search to washes and other areas below the mine, as well as back along the road. Even though material is comparatively scarce in those areas, it still could be worth your time.

Rockhounds are able to find a wealth of nice mineral specimens on the dumps, hillsides and washes throughout the area. One can obtain red, brown and yellow jasper, colorful agate and, in addition, some beautiful blue and white rhombohedral calcite crystals often found clinging to boulders. On the dumps, there is chrysocolla, malachite and even some hematite. Most of the malachite and chrysocolla are nothing more than stains, but some might be nice for mineral collections, especially if the color is good. Take enough time to properly explore this interesting spot. DO NOT enter any shafts and always be on the lookout for nails, glass and other such hazards associated with abandoned mines.

Exploring the Area Around the Now Abandoned Alvord Gold Mine

ALVORD MOUNTAINS

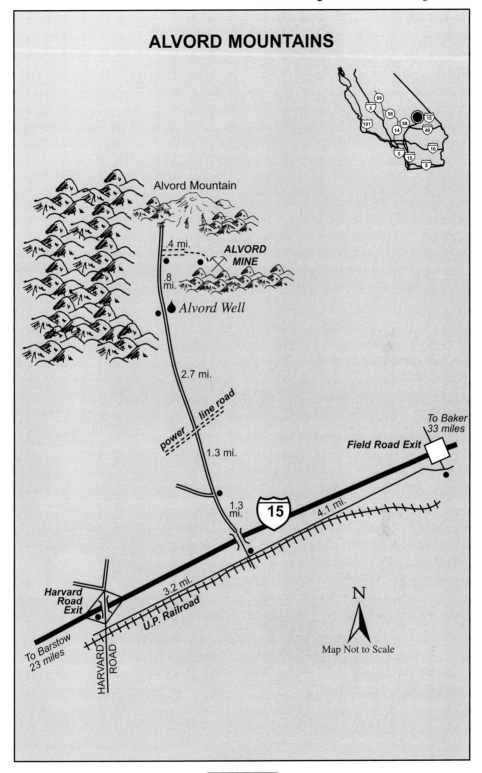

Alvord Mountain

.4 mi.

ALVORD MINE

.8 mi.

Alvord Well

2.7 mi.

power line road

1.3 mi.

To Baker 33 miles

Field Road Exit

1.3 mi.

15

4.1 mi.

Harvard Road Exit

3.2 mi.

U.P. Railroad

To Barstow 23 miles

HARVARD ROAD

N

Map Not to Scale

FIELD ROAD

These two collecting sites, on opposite sides of Interstate Highway 15, offer the rockhound a good variety of collectibles. To get to Site A, take the Field Road Exit, which is about 30 miles east of Barstow and 33 miles west of Baker. Go south, then east and then south again 1.4 miles, as shown on the map, to the railroad tracks. This is famous Field Siding, which, at one time, was one of the desert's best locations for finding beautiful jasper, agate, jasp-agate and occasional petrified wood.

Site A is expansive, extending south all the way from the highway in the north to south of the railroad tracks. The jasper occurs in a wide range of bright colors. The agate and wood occur in shades of brown and tan. Much of the material near the road has been taken, making it necessary to do some hiking to find worthwhile quantities. Most of what can be found tends to be small, but has nice colors and patterns.

Site B seems to have a little more available, even though, as was the case at Site A, specimens are generally small. To get there, return to Interstate Highway 15, and go north 2 miles to the southern edge of the gem field. Throughout the hills, on either side of the road, extending for at least another mile, you should be able to gather jasper, agate and jasp-agate in a wide variety of colors and patterns, as well as a rare piece of petrified wood. This site is also extensive, and, as was the case before, it is generally beneficial to hike away from the road in order to find larger pieces and better concentrations.

Whether at Site A or Site B, if you do any extensive hiking, do not lose your bearings. Even though the locations are near a major highway, it is very easy to get disoriented. Remember that this is a desert location, and it is not recommended that you hike any appreciable distance during the scorching summer months.

Site B

FIELD ROAD

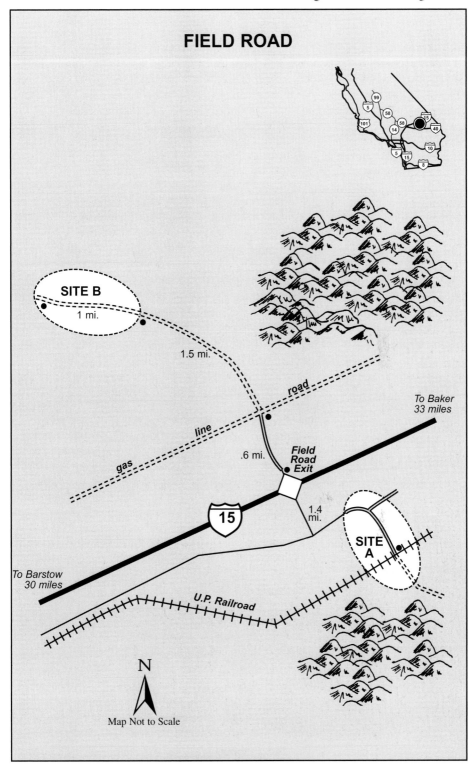

SITE B

1 mi.

1.5 mi.

road

line

gas

.6 mi.

Field
Road
Exit

To Baker
33 miles

15

To Barstow
30 miles

1.4
mi.

SITE
A

U.P. Railroad

N

Map Not to Scale

TOLTEC MINE

Both the Toltec Turquoise Mine and the little talc mine offer the collector some fine mineral specimens. To get there, take the Halloran Springs Exit from Interstate Highway 15, which is about 12 miles east of Baker. From there, head north on the paved road 6.5 miles to where you will encounter the talc prospect, on the right. At the talc mine, rockhounds can obtain brilliant white chunks of that very soft mineral, some of which is great for carving. In addition, many pieces can be found with black, fern-like pyrolusite dendrites. The dendrites make excellent display pieces.

The best dendrites are usually found by splitting the talc along natural fracture lines. Be advised that there is a very deep shaft in the middle of the dumps, which, at time of publication, was fenced off, but be very careful when collecting around it.

At the Toltec, you can find small, but beautifully colored, turquoise chips. To get there from the talc mine, continue about 0.8 miles, as shown on the map, to the where the paved road proceeds up the mountain to the relay station. At that point, very rough ruts will be seen continuing straight ahead. Follow them another 2.3 miles, turn right, and go another 0.2 miles to the road's end. Four-wheel drive is probably not necessary, but only rugged, high-clearance vehicles should attempt the drive. At the final mileage, is a great place to camp, and it puts you at the base of the trail leading to the old Toltec Turquoise Mine.

It is suggested that you park there and hike the approximately 0.25 miles to the dumps rather than trying to drive around the mountain on the faint and almost impassable ruts shown on the map. Take a hand trowel, small screen, a pair of tweezers and a bottle in which to place your gemstones. As you dig through the dumps, the tiny bright blue chips are easily spotted in the light gray soil, and with some patient work, you should be able to gather a good quantity in a short amount of time.

If there is any indication that collecting is no longer allowed, do not trespass. In addition, do not enter any shafts, since they are dangerous.

The Trail to Toltec

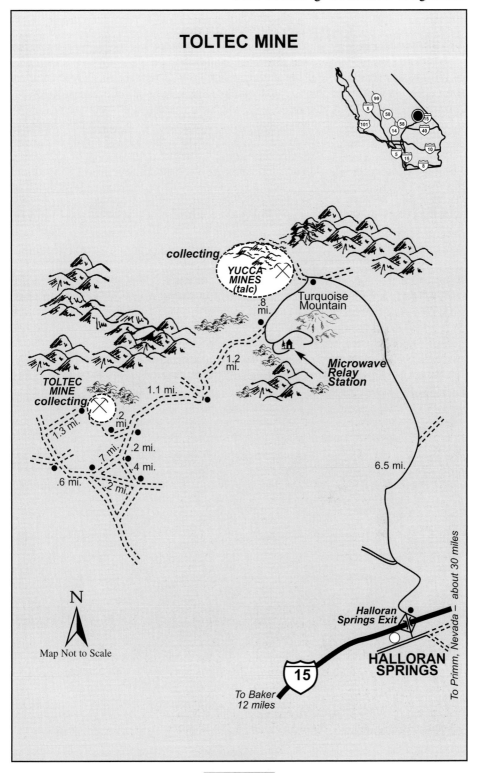

ZABRISKIE STATION OPAL

All or part of this site may be inside the newly formed Ibex Hills Wilderness Area. This will be a BLM administered region, as determined by the California Desert Protection Act of 1994. Hobby rock collecting is allowed, but certain restrictions apply. Be sure to read the Introduction for more information.

Precious and common opal can be found near the small town of Tecopa. To get there, drive 47.7 miles north from Baker on State Highway 127 to the Tecopa turnoff. Continue north another 2.1 miles to the ruins of Zabriskie Station, where you should turn left, and go about 0.2 miles into the unusual gray mud hills.

The opal is found in tiny tubes concealed within hard clay concretions embedded in the hills. Most of the tubes are very thin, no more than an inch long, a fraction of an inch in diameter, and very little of the opal contains fire. Be patient since every now and then colorful fiery specimens are discovered. Look for indications of previous digging for clues as to where you should start. Just north of the mud hills, scattered randomly throughout the terrain, rockhounds can find pieces of common opal, some of which is colorful, but little contains fire.

View of Previous Diggings in the Hillside

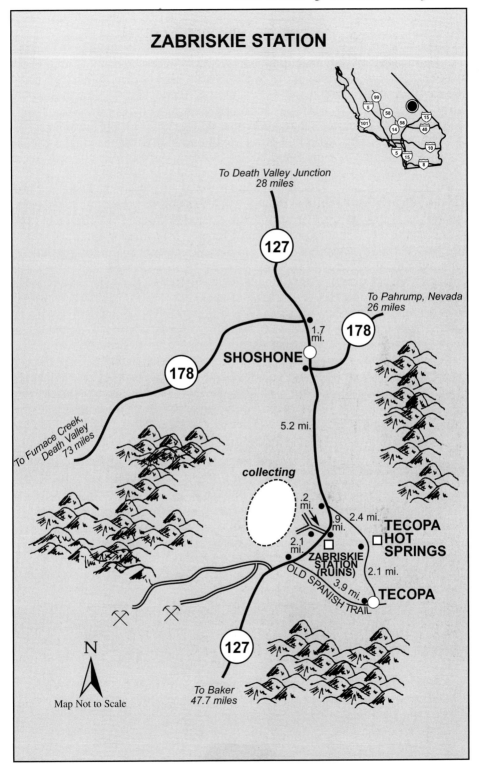

ZABRISKIE STATION

To Death Valley Junction
28 miles

127

To Pahrump, Nevada
26 miles

178

1.7 mi.

SHOSHONE

178

To Furnace Creek,
Death Valley
73 miles

5.2 mi.

collecting

.2 mi.

.9 mi.

2.4 mi.

TECOPA HOT SPRINGS

2.1 mi.

2.1 mi.

ZABRISKIE
STATION
(RUINS)

OLD SPANISH TRAIL

3.9 mi.

TECOPA

N

Map Not to Scale

127

To Baker
47.7 miles

TECOPA MINERALS

This vast collecting area has been well-known amongst rockhounds for decades. It is one of those places where a little luck is nice, due to the sheer acreage encompassed by the site's boundaries. Be advised that the road going through the collecting area is bounded on both sides by the Kingston Range Wilderness Area making it mandatory that you do not drive off the main route. It will be necessary to park just off the road and hike to wherever you choose to go. This should not present a major problem since that is the way most collecting was done here even before the formation of the wilderness area.

To get to the site's eastern edge, start where Old Spanish Trail Road and Furnace Creek Road intersect, about 1.5 miles east of the small town of Tecopa. From there, go right onto Furnace Creek Road and travel 7.8 miles to the talc mine road where you should turn right (west). After having gone 2.7 miles, the first of many roads leading to the old talc mine heads off to the left. If, and only if, the mine is abandoned when you visit, you can pick up a few interesting samples of talc. Material is scattered all over the terrain surrounding the mine.

Continuing along the main road about 2.5 miles farther you leave the mining area and you should bear right at the fork onto the rougher road leading alongside the Kingston Range Wilderness Area boundary. From that point, and continuing at least another 5 miles, specimens of petrified wood, agate and jasper can be found on either side of the road. Just park anywhere you feel lucky. Be sure to pull off far enough to allow other vehicles easy passage and then simply hike in any direction looking for the wood, agate and jasper. When you have explored one spot, get back in your vehicle and repeat the process as many times as you desire. As is always the case in places like this, concentrations vary greatly. Just be patient and willing to do a little walking, and you surely will gather an acceptable quantity of these nice collectibles. Remember to read the Introduction for more information about collecting within the wilderness area.

TECOPA

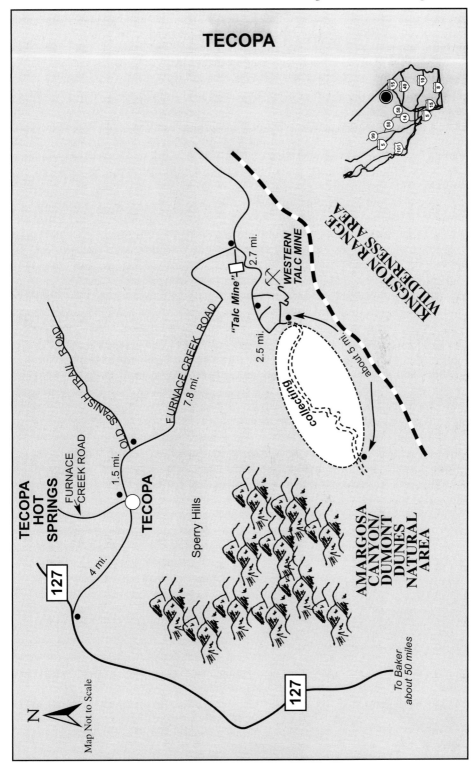

TECOPA HOT SPRINGS

127

FURNACE CREEK ROAD

OLD SPANISH TRAIL ROAD

4 mi.

1.5 mi.

TECOPA

FURNACE CREEK ROAD

7.8 mi.

2.7 mi.

"Talc Mine"

WESTERN TALC MINE

2.5 mi.

collecting

about 5 mi.

KINGSTON RANGE WILDERNESS AREA

Sperry Hills

AMARGOSA CANYON/ DUMONT DUNES NATURAL AREA

127

To Baker about 50 miles

N

Map Not to Scale

KINGSTON MOUNTAIN

Beautiful quartz crystals can be found throughout the portion of the Kingston Mountains shown on the accompanying map. Most are clear or milky, but some are prize amethyst varieties. The main road to the collecting area is well-graded, but steep in places. Rugged vehicles should have no problem getting to the designated parking spot. There is an old road leading off to the right from the main one into a wide box canyon. It enters the Kingston Range Wilderness Area and no vehicles are allowed to proceed any farther. The hike is not bad, and there is plenty to be found along the way to the primary collecting spot.

To get to the Kingston Mountain collecting site, take State Highway 127 north from Baker 47.7 miles to the Old Spanish Trail Highway, which is the turnoff to Tecopa. Go 5.4 miles and then fork right onto Furnace Creek Road, traveling another 18 steep miles to an old mine on the left. From there, near the summit, continue 1.1 more miles to where faint ruts will be spotted on the right, leading toward the mountains, this being the route to the site.

The best collecting is accomplished by carefully examining the boulders and rock at the base of the mountains, but crystals can be found just about anywhere from the main road all the way to the foothills, especially in the washes.

Look for single specimens throughout the wash leading toward the mountains and carefully inspect any boulders you encounter for cavities or seams. You will need a sturdy hammer, chisel, goggles and gloves to split the tough host rock, but your work will frequently be rewarded. Turning the soft sand in the wash with a garden rake or hand trowel will also sometimes be helpful in exposing otherwise buried crystals.

There are veins throughout the mountains at the head of the wash, and at one time, there was an amethyst claim there. Be patient and willing to do some work, and you should return home with many fine specimens.

This is a scenic location, but not advisable during the winter, since snow can close the road and/or make collecting either very unpleasant or downright impossible. Ice can remain on the crystal-bearing rock for quite a few months after severe storms, so late spring or summer are generally the best months to look for beautiful Kingston Mountain crystals.

Splitting the Host Rock

KINGSTON MOUNTAIN

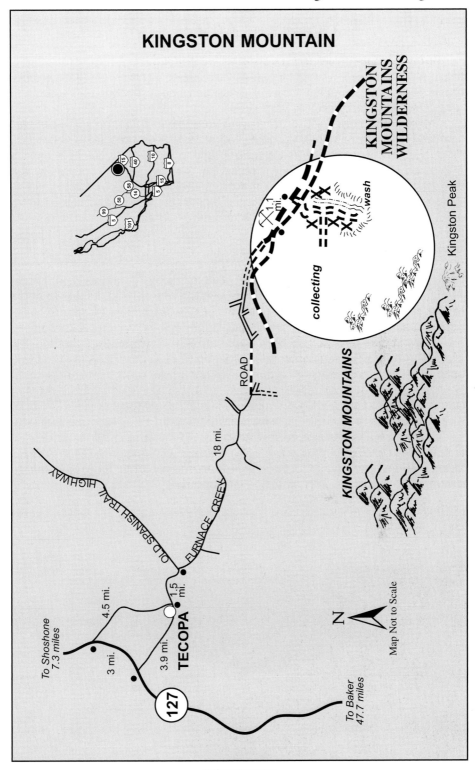

KINGSTON MOUNTAINS WILDERNESS

KINGSTON MOUNTAINS

Kingston Peak

collecting

wash

1.1 mi.

ROAD

18 mi.

FURNACE CREEK

OLD SPANISH TRAIL HIGHWAY

To Shoshone
7.3 miles

4.5 mi.

3 mi.

3.9 mi.

1.5 mi.

TECOPA

127

To Baker
47.7 miles

N

Map Not to Scale

EL PASO MOUNTAINS OPAL AND FOSSILS

One of the few places in California where precious opal can be found with any reliability is in the western part of the El Paso Mountains. There are two fee locations, in particular, which provide an opportunity for rockhounds to search for that highly prized, fiery gemstones.

To get to the center of this scenic and productive region, go north on State Highway 14 approximately 27 miles from Mojave to the "Elevation 3,000 Feet" sign. From there, proceed exactly 1 mile to the turnoff. There is usually a sign on the east, designating that to be the route to Opal Canyon, but whether the sign is there or not, the turn is easy to spot from the pavement. Follow the well-graded dirt road 0.3 miles, bear right, and go another 1.2 miles to another intersection. Be advised that the road goes through a portion of Red Rock Canyon State Park and there is no mineral or fossil collecting allowed within the park boundaries.

At the intersection, go left 1 more mile to where you will encounter a group of signs and a major fork in the road. One of the signs points right to the Barnett Opal Mine and another directs rockhounds to the left toward the Nowak Opal Mine. At time of publication, the Barnett was opened on a regular basis, primarily on weekends and a minimal fee is charged to work on the claim. The Nowak has not been as regular with its collecting schedule, but if you tire of the Barnett Mine, you might want to double back to see if it is open. Both of these mines are famous throughout the southwest for the often spectacular, fire-filled opal that can be found there. Don't be mislead, though. Obtaining top quality gem material takes immense work, patience and a lot of luck. The opal is there for those who are willing to break up the host rock with sledgehammers, chisels and gads in an effort to expose opal-filled cavities. Be sure to take gloves, goggles, a lot to drink and a willingness to work. At both mines, there is always someone there to get you started and to demonstrate the proper techniques.

Fork to Sites D and E

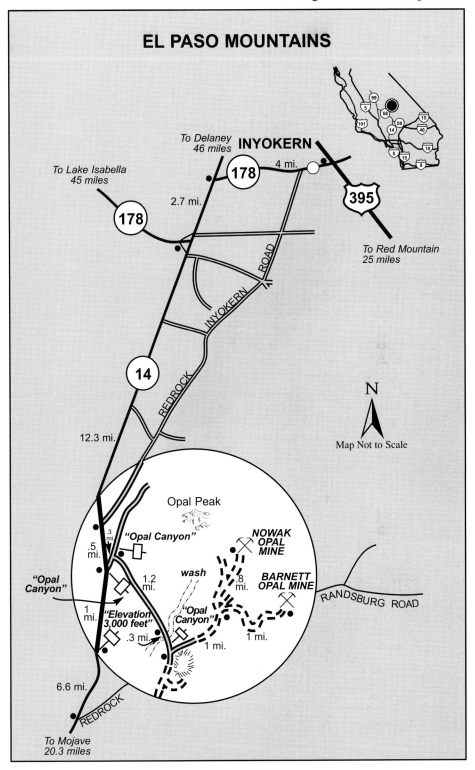

EL PASO MOUNTAINS

To Delaney
46 miles

INYOKERN

To Lake Isabella
45 miles

178

4 mi.

178

2.7 mi.

395

To Red Mountain
25 miles

INYOKERN ROAD

14

REDROCK

12.3 mi.

N

Map Not to Scale

Opal Peak

.3 mi.

"Opal Canyon"

.5 mi.

NOWAK OPAL MINE

"Opal Canyon"

1.2 mi.

wash

.8 mi.

BARNETT OPAL MINE

RANDSBURG ROAD

1 mi.

"Elevation 3,000 feet"

"Opal Canyon"

.3 mi.

1 mi.

1 mi.

6.6 mi.

REDROCK

To Mojave
20.3 miles

STEAM WELL

Agate, chalcedony and tons of exceptionally colorful opalite can be found at the three sites shown on the accompanying map. The problem with collecting at this otherwise highly productive location is that it now completely lies within the boundaries of the newly created BLM Golden Valley Wilderness Area. For that reason, it should only be considered to those who are in top physical condition and have a sound knowledge of desert survival—everybody else is now been eliminated from making the trip! It is recommended that you do not attempt getting to these sites due to the hazards involved, but that decision is up to you.

If you want to make the trek, take the Trona Road turnoff from U.S. Highway 395, about 1 mile north of Red Mountain and 25 miles north of Kramer Junction. Proceed 1.3 miles and then follow well-graded Steam Well Road east another 6.9 miles. Steam Well Road forms the southern boundary of the wilderness, so regions to your left (north) are in the wilderness and only accessible by hiking. Park at the road intersection, as illustrated on the accompanying map, and hike about 2.3 miles. At that mileage there is an intersection and you should go left about 1 more mile to the first of the three collecting sites. Be sure to take plenty of water and a backpack or sturdy collecting bag within which to haul your minerals.

At Site A, look for quite a distance in all directions for agate and chert. Blue agate is the most-prized, especially that with moss inclusions.

Site B is only 0.5 miles farther along (easy for me to say!) and is, by far, the most prolific of the locations. It features a ridge entirely composed of colorful opalite and the road passes only a few feet south of it. The opalite can be removed directly from the cliffs or picked up throughout the lowlands below. Agate and chert can be found throughout the upper flatlands on either side of the road.

Site C is centered around the easily spotted gray hills to the northeast. In and around those conspicuous mounds, stretching all the way back to the main road, one can find agate. Some of these agate pieces contain interesting inclusions which can be used to make fascinating cabochons and other polished pieces. Do some digging in the mounds for the most-sizable specimens.

STEAM WELL

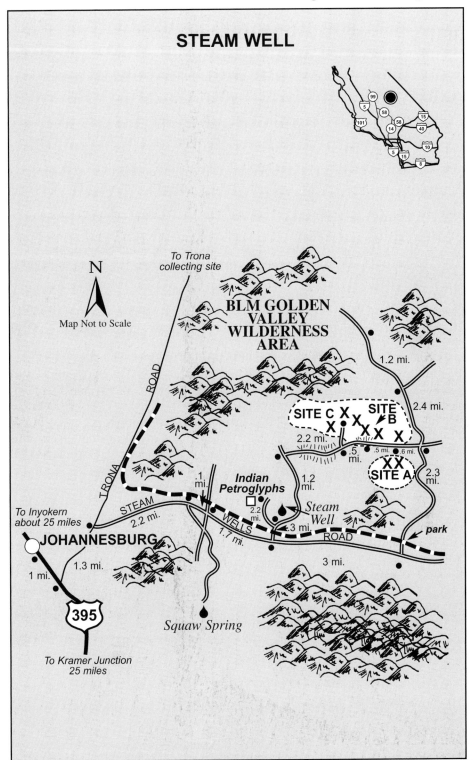

BEDROCK SPRING

All three of these locations boast nice agate, chalcedony and jasper. Due to some severely washed out roads, these locations should only be of interest to rockhounds with a lot of patience and a willingness to do some walking, and a sturdy vehicle with four-wheel drive is advisable if not mandatory.

To get to Site A, go north on Trona Road 6.7 miles from where it intersects U.S. Highway 395. At that point, turn east on Savoy Road and proceed 5.1 miles to where the dirt road starts to rapidly deteriorate. This entire road forms the northern boundary of the Golden Valley Wilderness Area, so there is no driving to the south. The route to Bedrock Springs intersects from the right, but you should continue straight ahead. It is strongly advisable that you park there, and hike the remaining distance, even if you have a four-wheel drive vehicle. The road is severely washed out and there are not many places to turn around. If you decide to continue driving, you will be somewhat committed for at least 0.3 miles, and keep in mind, this is an extremely remote location in which to get stuck.

The hike isn't bad from the Bedrock Spring turnoff, but you do have to walk in and out of washed out and rocky areas. Go about 0.5 miles and, on the left will be a little canyon. At the far end of that canyon is a tiny gray hill locally known as Agate Hill which is randomly covered with small chunks of very colorful agate and chalcedony. If you feel like carrying a shovel with you, digging into the soft soil might prove to be very productive. The agate is clear, often filled with delicate dendritic inclusions. There is also some nice green jasper to be found here, so be on the lookout.

Site B is approximately 0.5 miles farther along the main road. It is centered around a dark hill at the end of yet another side canyon on the left. On and around that hill, rockhounds can find more agate and jasper, as well as some nice, layered sardonyx. Site B does not seem to be as productive as Site A, but the variety is better. Remember, when visiting these two sites, that you must walk slightly uphill to get back to your car. Take some extra water and a sturdy bag in which to haul whatever you find. Most importantly, don't tackle a hike you may not be able to accomplish.

Site C is more accessible, but since it next to Trona Road, much of the surface material has been picked up over the years. Colorful jasper can be found by those willing to do a little hiking away from the pavement, but nothing is overly plentiful here anymore. To get there, return to Trona Road, go north about 2.3 miles and park. The jasper can be found on both sides of the road, but tends to be a little more plentiful to the east.

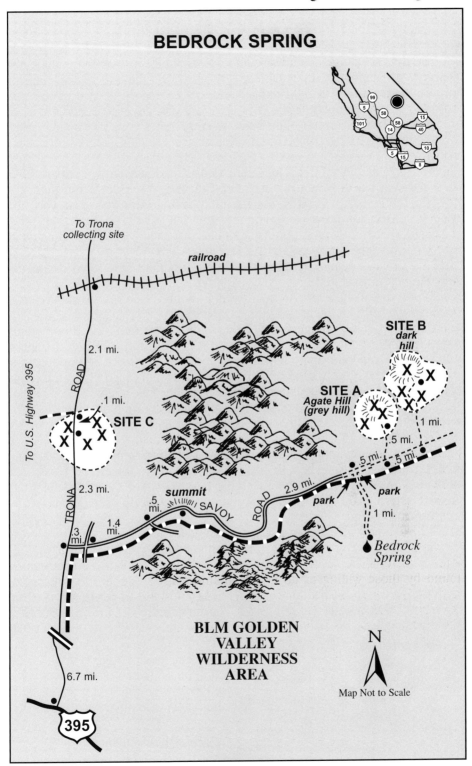

BEDROCK SPRING

To Trona
collecting site

railroad

SITE B
dark
hill

SITE A
Agate Hill
(grey hill)

SITE C

2.1 mi.

.1 mi.

X X
X X

To U.S. Highway 395

ROAD

TRONA

2.3 mi.

summit

SAVOY

.5
mi.

3
mi.

1.4
mi.

2.9 mi.

park

park

1 mi.

.5 mi.

.5 mi. .5 mi.

1 mi.

*Bedrock
Spring*

6.7 mi.

**BLM GOLDEN
VALLEY
WILDERNESS
AREA**

N

Map Not to Scale

395

RAINBOW RIDGE

The six sites described here offer rockhounds a seemingly unlimited supply of top quality opalite, agate and jasper. To get the best specimens from any of the localities, it is usually necessary to use hard rock equipment, including sledgehammers, gads, chisels, gloves and goggles, in order to work the mineral-bearing seams. For those who do not want to engage in such strenuous work, though, there are a lot of small specimens lying around, some of which are very nice.

Access to all the sites is achieved by taking the Randsburg-Inyokern Road 2.7 miles west from where it intersects U.S. Highway 395. From there, go south 1.1 miles, turn right, cross the railroad tracks and then proceed left 0.5 miles. At that point, turn right, go another 0.5 miles, and then drive left to the easily spotted diggings another 0.3 miles up the hill. This is designated as Site A on the map.

Site A boasts opalite in veins and float. The colors include yellow, green, orange, pink and white in a variety of patterns and combinations. Some also contains moss inclusions. At nearby Sites B and C, one can obtain more opalite, especially in and around the excavations.

To get to Site D, it is necessary to go approximately 0.4 miles in a sandy wash. Be sure your vehicle can make it before heading in. At the given mileage, you can find agate featuring a spectacular swirled red and orange variety. Look for quite a distance throughout the area, especially in the easily spotted areas where previous rockhounds have been working.

Site E is yet another very productive opalite location. It is reached by returning to the main road, heading south 1.8 miles, and then turning right another 1.5 miles to where excavations can be spotted on the hillside. Site E boasts good quality opalite, often filed with delicate moss inclusions, and colors tend to be in shades of green.

Site F is the famous Rainbow Ridge jasper location. It is a remarkable deposit, offering top quality jasper in an amazing variety of vivid colors and interesting patterns. This is a private claim, held by the Indian Wells Gem & Mineral Society, which, at time of publication, was open to collectors. Let the club know how many people are going and how long you will stay. This is so

they can submit that information with their annual assessment affidavit. Be sure to send that information to the Indian Wells Gem & Mineral Society, P.O. Box 1481, Ridgecrest, CA 93555 or you can e-mail them at erich@ridgecrest.ca.us. In addition, only hand tools are allowed at Rainbow Ridge. No power equipment or explosives can be used.

Gathering Specimens at Site A

RAINBOW RIDGE

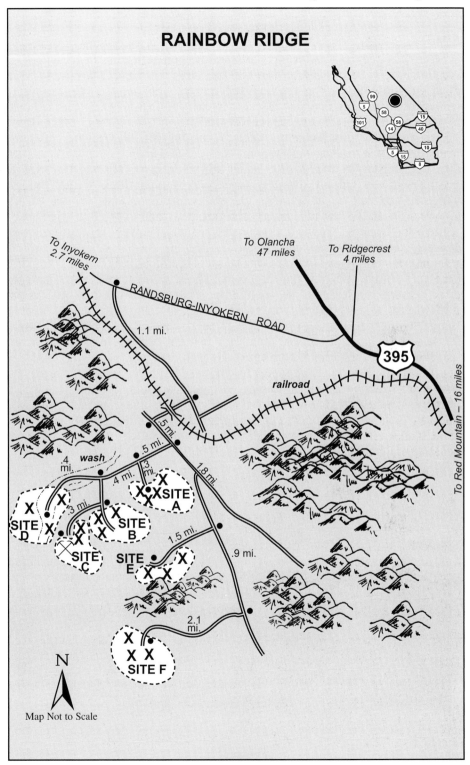

To Inyokern
2.7 miles

To Olancha
47 miles

To Ridgecrest
4 miles

RANDSBURG-INYOKERN ROAD

1.1 mi.

395

railroad

To Red Mountain – 16 miles

.5 mi.

.4 mi.

wash

.5 mi.

.3 mi.

.4 mi.

1.8 mi.

X
X X SITE A

.3 mi.

X
X

SITE D

X

X X
X X

SITE B

X X
SITE C

SITE E
X
X X

1.5 mi.

X
X

.9 mi.

2.1 mi.

X
X X
SITE F

N

Map Not to Scale

SHEEP SPRINGS

The Sheep Springs collecting site offers high quality moss agate and moss opalite, in good quantities. In fact, a large portion of the hill, directly in front of where you must park, is covered with outstanding material ranging in size from pebbles to large boulders. Most is white, with black dendrites, but some is pale blue, which is the most highly prized.

To get to this prolific area, take the Randsburg-Inyokern Road southeast from Inyokern 2.7 miles. At that point, a dirt road will be seen, intersecting on the right. Follow that road 4.8 miles and then turn right, going another 2.9 miles into the hills. At the given mileage, bear left at the fork, go 0.2 miles, and then bear left again, traveling 0.3 miles farther to Sheep Springs. Park anywhere near the given mileage, but please do not stop or camp near the springs themselves. This is a very important water supply for local wildlife, and your presence could have a negative effect.

From the spring, a faint trail can be seen heading up into the hills. Agate veins are found at higher elevations for those wishing to extract material directly from its place in the mountain. That requires substantial work, including a steep hike. If you want to try working the seams, take a sledgehammer, gads and chisels, as well as gloves and goggles. Be prepared for some hard labor in order to obtain the best the site has to offer.

Those who make the effort are usually well rewarded.

If such an task does not appeal to you, jasper, opalite and black agate are scattered throughout the lowlands. A small amount of petrified wood, primarily near the sandstone outcrops. Just walk throughout the little hills and the lower washes, keeping an eye out for the easily spotted cutting materials. Most of the opalite and jasper are very colorful and can be used to make exquisite polished pieces.

View of the Collecting Site

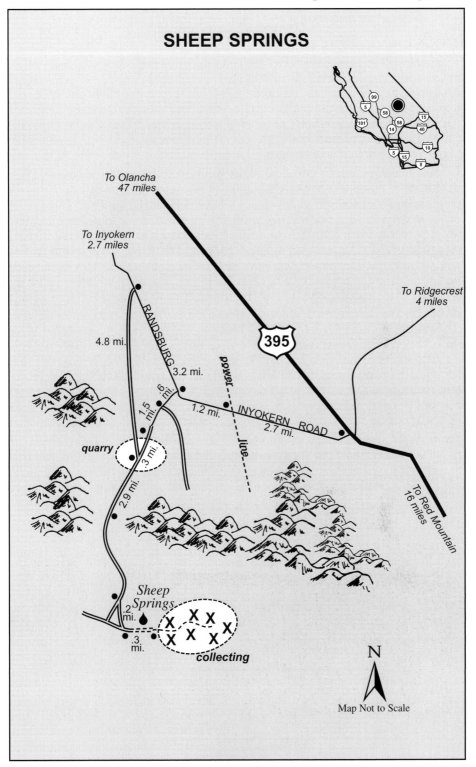

SHEEP SPRINGS

To Olancha
47 miles

To Inyokern
2.7 miles

RANDSBURG

To Ridgecrest
4 miles

4.8 mi.

3.2 mi.

power

395

.6 mi.

1.5 mi.

1.2 mi.

INYOKERN ROAD
2.7 mi.

line

quarry

.3 mi.

2.9 mi.

To Red Mountain
16 miles

Sheep
Springs

.2 mi.

X X X
X X X

.3 mi.

collecting

N

Map Not to Scale

TRONA ONYX

Some of the most colorful onyx available anywhere in California can be found at the two locations illustrated on the accompanying map. Both of these sites were at one time fee locations, but their current status is uncertain. At time of publication, both appeared to be abandoned and there was no indication that the original claims were being maintained. If there is any indication that collecting is not allowed or a fee is again required to gather material, please honor the rights of the claim holders.

Site A is the famous Onyx Mine, featuring banded and swirled travertine, in shades of green, brown, red, gold and white. Look on the dumps for loose chunks, or attack the mountain of onyx itself with sledgehammer, chisels and gads. To get there, go north on Trona Road from the Trona Library, 17.9 miles to Nadeau Road. Turn left after 3.1 miles, and then turn left another 1.3 miles to where the road is completely eroded away. When the Onyx Mine was in operation, the road was well maintained, but, now, it is necessary to bear left and circle around the backside, a distance of about 2.2 miles. There is a large windmill and a sizable building at the mine. They can be seen from quite a distance, providing a good landmark to drive toward. The onyx-bearing hill is easily spotted in the center of the abandoned buildings.

Site B is not overly productive, but does offer a few specimens of garnet in granite, honey onyx, white onyx, jasper and agate. The collecting is done throughout a vast region on both sides of Nadeau Road, starting at the highway and continuing about 2 miles north.

Site C is the Aquarius Onyx Mine. Most of what is found there occurs in tones of honey, brown and white, much of which displays beautiful lace patterns. To get there, go south from where Nadeau Road intersects Trona Road 4.1 miles and then turn right onto the dirt road. Follow that road 1.5

miles to the broken down gate, marking what used to be the entrance of the Aquarius Onyx Mine. The onyx deposit is straight ahead and then to the right.

Collecting at Site A

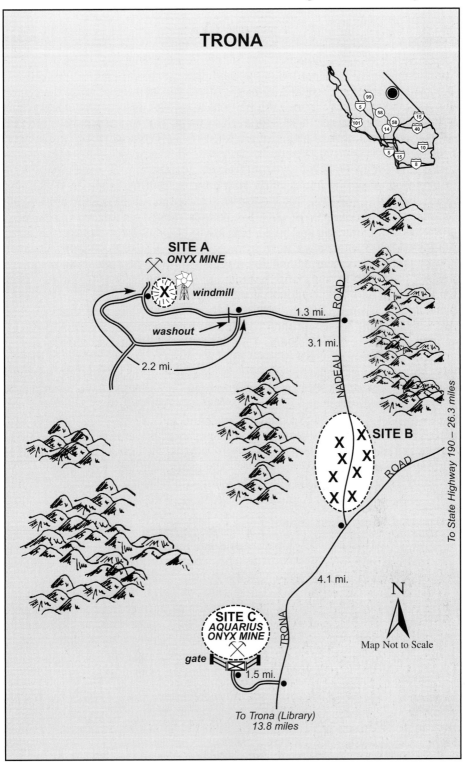

TRONA

SITE A
ONYX MINE

windmill

washout

1.3 mi.

3.1 mi.

2.2 mi.

NADEAU ROAD

X **SITE B**
X **X**
X **X**
X
X **X**

ROAD

To State Highway 190 – 26.3 miles

4.1 mi.

N

Map Not to Scale

TRONA

SITE C
*AQUARIUS
ONYX MINE*

gate

1.5 mi.

To Trona (Library)
13.8 miles

BALLARAT

Ballarat was once famous for its rich gold mines but nowadays it is better known amongst rockhounds for the beautiful onyx that can be found there. The three locations discussed here will allow you to sample what the region has to offer. To get to Site A, take Ballarat Road east from Trona Road, which is about 21.8 miles north of Trona. Starting at that intersection, travel 3.5 miles to the small town of Ballarat and then turn north on Wingate Road. After 1.1 miles, turn right onto Happy Canyon Road (which may not be marked) and go another 3.7 miles into the mountains. Be advised that Happy Canyon Road forms the southern boundary of the newly formed Surprise Canyon Wilderness Area, thereby prohibiting vehicle travel north from the road. The last stretch is quite steep, but the road isn't too bad. A rugged vehicle should have no problems making the trip and four-wheel drive shouldn't be necessary unless the road is wet.

At the given mileage, look for a rock slide on the right that being the center of Site A. Throughout that slide, one can find tons of white and black onyx, as well as an exceptionally nice orange, banded variety. The white and black material is nice, but the orange is the prize. Some of it, if the colors are rich enough and it isn't grainy, can be used to make exquisite clock faces, carvings, spheres, bookends and other larger polished pieces.

Tons of quality material can be found throughout the rock slide, but if you want to go after the deposits themselves, it is necessary to carefully scramble to the top of the rubble. If you do try your hand at removing the onyx from the seams, you will need a sledgehammer, gads, chisels, gloves, goggles and plenty of energy. There is so much to be found in the rock slide, though, that it really doesn't seem necessary to expend so much energy in an effort to simply get more of the same. Be very careful when on the rock slide, since nothing is very stable, making it very easy to slip and fall.

More onyx can be found randomly scattered throughout the wash at Site B, which is 0.4 miles south of Ballarat, as illustrated on the map. This is the least

productive of these three locations, but is still worth a stop while in the area.

One-half mile farther south, more onyx can be found scatted throughout the low-lying hills. This is labeled as Site C, and the quantity is nothing like at Site A, but the variety tends to be greater. Plan to do some diligent hiking if you want to find sizable chunks. With patience, and the willingness to spend some time here, you will certainly be well rewarded for your effort.

Searching for Marble at Site A

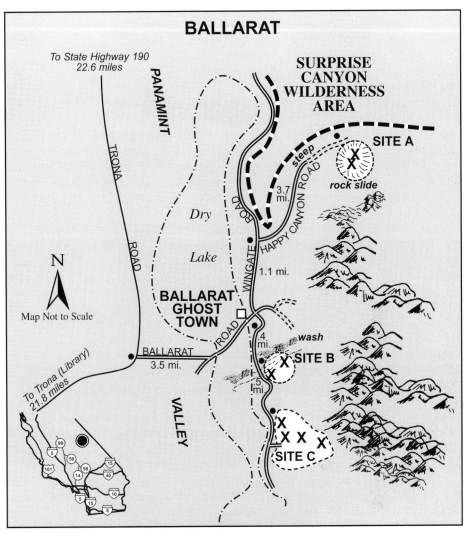

BALLARAT

To State Highway 190
22.6 miles

PANAMINT

TRONA

ROAD

SURPRISE CANYON WILDERNESS AREA

steep

3.7 mi.

HAPPY CANYON ROAD

WINGATE

SITE A

rock slide

Dry

Lake

1.1 mi.

N

Map Not to Scale

BALLARAT GHOST TOWN

ROAD

.4 mi.

wash

SITE B

X X

.5 mi.

BALLARAT
3.5 mi.

To Trona (Library)
21.8 miles

VALLEY

SITE C

X
X X X

99
5
58
58
101
14
15
40
5
10
15
8

Parked at Site A

OLANCHA FOSSILS

This site is situated within the boundaries of the Coso Range Wilderness Area and is thereby protected by the California Desert Protection Act of 1994. Hobby rock collecting is allowed, but certain restrictions apply. Be sure to read the Introduction for more information.

The location offers collectors an opportunity to find some very nice fossilized bone specimens, and has provided paleontologists with numerous, well-preserved mammal fossils over the years. Bone chips and fragments are fairly easy to find, but complete skeletons are rare. Remnants of mice, rabbits, wild dogs, horses, ancient pigs and a variety of other animals have been discovered weathering out of the fossil-bearing strata, only a few miles east of Olancha. You will need a vehicle equipped with four-wheel drive, or you must be willing to hike about 2 miles. Do not attempt this trip during the scorching summer months, and be sure to take plenty of supplies in the event you are delayed.

To get there, take State Highway 190 about 5.9 miles east from where it intersects U.S. Highway 395. At that point, is a large wash heading southeast from the pavement, as illustrated on the map. The fossils are embedded in rock within the canyons and foothills of the easily spotted Coso Mountains. If you choose to drive, be cautious leaving the pavement and when getting into the wash. There are some steep drops and it will take careful planning to determine exactly where to enter. The wilderness boundary is slightly less than 1 mile in from the pavement and you are not allowed to drive farther. In any event, you will have to do some hiking whether it be from the highway or from wherever you park along the way. Be certain you are physically capable of making the entire trek, be sure to take plenty to drink and take a backpack for carrying specimens. The collecting takes place alongside the wash about 1.7 miles from State Highway 190 where you see the sedimentary rock coming in contact with brown igneous material. The fossils tend to occur in the associated tan sandstone within the upper portions of the sedimentary deposits.

The bones are sometimes partially exposed, sticking out of the sandstone, due to the forces of erosion. In addition, many good specimens can be found in the lower areas, having already been completely weathered out. You can either use small tools and screens to examine the loose soil, or heavier equipment to dig into the fossil-bearing sandstone directly.

The fossil-bearing strata continues throughout much of the foothills and into many of the little adjacent canyons. If you have the time, a search of some of the less accessible portions of the Coso Mountains might prove to be very fruitful.

Some of the auxiliary canyons have produced well preserved jaws, teeth and complete bones. If you should unearth an entire skeleton, it would be very helpful if you note, as accurately as possible, where it was found and report it to a university. That would allow them to conduct further study, if it is in fact a significant find.

Wash Leading to the Site

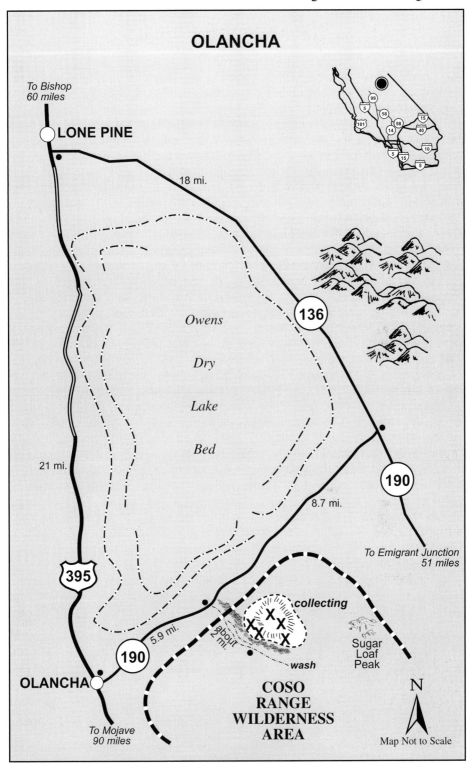

OLANCHA

To Bishop
60 miles

LONE PINE

18 mi.

Owens

Dry

Lake

Bed

136

21 mi.

190

395

8.7 mi.

To Emigrant Junction
51 miles

collecting

X X
X
X X

Sugar
Loaf
Peak

about ⅜ mi.

wash

5.9 mi.

190

OLANCHA

To Mojave
90 miles

COSO
RANGE
WILDERNESS
AREA

N

Map Not to Scale

CERRO GORDO FOSSILS

In spite of the fact that the Cerro Gordo Mine produced countless dollars in zinc, lead and silver during the last part of the nineteenth century, those old mines are now closed. What remains now are virtually all on private land thereby unavailable to rockhounds. Interestingly, there are a lot of fossils embedded within the cliffs surrounding the remnants of Cerro Gordo and most of those deposits are on public lands. What can be found includes nicely formed ammonites, pelecypods and even shark's teeth.

If you want to take this scenic trip into the past, start in Lone Pine. From town, go south on U.S. Highway 395 only a short distance to State Highway 136. Turn east (left) and proceed another 13 miles to Keeler and the intersection of Cerro Gordo Road. Follow Cerro Gordo Road as it rapidly climbs from the dry lake to the mountain summit. This is not a trip for underpowered vehicles or large ones and there are not a lot of good places to turn around along the way. Four-wheel drive is not necessary, but the trip is steep and winding.

Six miles up from State Highway 136 you will enter the Keeler Canyon Formation. Within its shale, tiny fossilized fusulinids and crinoids can be found. Nothing here is very large or well-preserved, but it makes a nice stopping point along the way. Cerro Gordo Summit is encountered just a little over 8 miles from State Highway 136, and at that point, you should turn left (northeast) onto the rough jeep tracks which follow along the upper ridge. Go only 0.1 miles and then turn left again. Drive 1 more mile to the trail that leads off to the north. This is called the Pipeline Trail and it is the route to the region's best fossil collecting. There is no good place to park here, so proceed about 0.1 miles farther to the wide "parking" area and simply walk back. Follow the pipeline trail about 0.5 miles to the dark gray shale deposits, primarily on the right side of the footpath.

Explore the shale for well-preserved ammonites, pelecypods and shark's teeth. Occasionally collectors encounter plant remains, corals and nautiloids, so be on the lookout.

When you tire of collecting, spend a little time in nearby Cerro Gordo. Even though mineral collecting is not readily available there, samples of what has come from the nearby mines can be viewed.

View Looking Back at the Dry Lake on the Road to Cerro Gordo

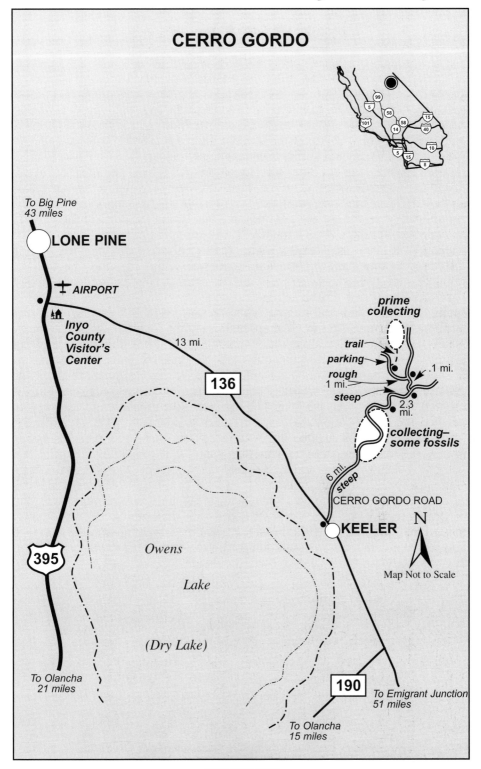

CERRO GORDO

To Big Pine
43 miles

LONE PINE

✈ AIRPORT

🏕 Inyo County Visitor's Center

13 mi.

136

prime collecting

trail

parking

rough
1 mi.

steep

.1 mi.

2.3 mi.

collecting–
some fossils

6 mi.

steep

CERRO GORDO ROAD

KEELER

N

Map Not to Scale

395

Owens

Lake

(Dry Lake)

To Olancha
21 miles

190

To Emigrant Junction
51 miles

To Olancha
15 miles

LONE PINE AMMONITES

Well-preserved, coiled ammonite fossils can be obtained from a very productive deposit located a relatively short distance northeast of Lone Pine. To get there, go north from Lone Pine on U.S. Highway 395 about 0.2 miles to where Narrow Gauge Road intersects from the east. Turn right, proceed 3 miles and bear left another 5.3 miles to Union Wash one of California's premiere ammonite locations. The roads are not too rough, but certainly not suitable for passenger cars. Rugged vehicles with adequate clearance are desirable, but four-wheel drive will not be needed to get this far.

At the given mileage, go right (east) onto Union Wash Road and travel another 1.7 miles. At that point there is a fork in the road marking where you should park. From there and continuing along Union Wash Road the primary ammonite collecting will be primarily on the south (right) side of the road. Be advised that the primary deposit is situated well above the road on the right in the dark gray limestone. If you want to scramble to the deposit, there is a very rough and steep trail leading to it about 0.1 miles farther along the way, but it is not recommended. Proper shoes and good physical fitness are required to safely make the climb and it really isn't necessary. So much material has been broken loose over time that great specimens can be found amongst the rubble and rock scattered below. In addition, examining and breaking up such pieces is much easier than attacking the tough deposits directly from the mountainside.

Carefully examine any of the limestone rock that lies at the base of the cliffs. The ammonites are actually black molds and do not contain any of the original shell material. That makes them a little tough to spot, but with practice, the identification process gets easier. Just be patient. Breaking up the tough limestone will expose fresh surfaces and thereby frequently makes finding the fascinating ancient creatures easier. The process will require that you use a sledgehammer and a few good-sized gads or chisels, but the extra effort might well pay dividends.

There are more ammonites about 1 more mile farther up Union Wash, but driving is not allowed since it is located within the boundaries of the newly formed Inyo Mountains Wilderness Area. The trek is uphill and tough, but if you feel like doing more exploration of the region and are properly equipped and physically fit, the hike might pay dividends.

*The
Lone Pine
Site*

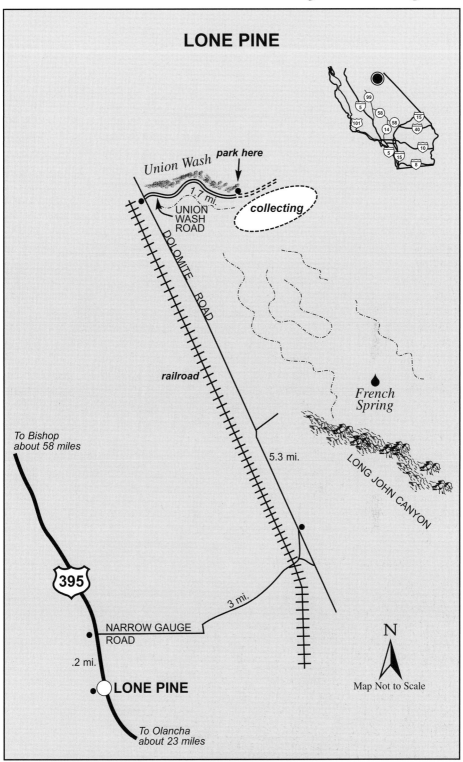

LONE PINE

park here

Union Wash

1.7 mi.

UNION WASH ROAD

collecting

DOLOMITE ROAD

railroad

French Spring

LONG JOHN CANYON

To Bishop
about 58 miles

5.3 mi.

395

3 mi.

NARROW GAUGE ROAD

.2 mi.

⦿ **LONE PINE**

To Olancha
about 23 miles

N

Map Not to Scale

TOPANGA FOSSILS

Nice fossilized clams can be found in this easily accessed site, next to Old Topanga Canyon Road, about 25 north of Los Angeles. In addition, collectors can obtain small ammonites, shark's teeth, turritella shells and other marine fossils, most of which are very well-preserved.

To get to this interesting location, take U.S. Highway 101 west from where it intersects Interstate Highway 5 for about 25.1 miles to the Las Virgenes Road Exit. Go south 3.1 miles to Mulholland Highway, then east 7.4 miles to Old Topanga Canyon Road. Turn right and proceed another 1.2 miles along that winding stretch of pavement, pulling off in the "parking area" on the right. The fossils are found in the cliffs next to the road. Look not only in the easiest accessed region within the "parking area," but also walk back along the road past the curve. Be very careful when hiking on the road, though. It is fairly well traveled and motorists aren't expecting to encounter pedestrians. In addition, be certain not to knock anything onto the pavement.

Specimens can often be found amongst the rubble beneath the banks and those are, by far, the easiest to gather. Just sort through the rock and debris with a little hand rake, trowel and a screen. The prize turritella shells come from a strata high on the cliffs, and signs of digging can be seen where previous collectors have worked. They are somewhat small, not measuring much over an inch in length, and it takes some patient work to find many. You also have to be very careful when removing them, since they tend to be very fragile. Complete specimens are tough to obtain, but chunks of the host rock containing a few of the coiled turritellas can make all the work worthwhile. The other fossils tend to be much easy to gather, due to their blackish color, which stands out against the lighter host soil.

Be advised that most of the cliffs are somewhat unstable, making it mandatory to be very cautious when working under an overhang or ledge. In addition, for the same reason, be most careful if you choose to do any climbing. It is important to note that most visitors to this location are extremely satisfied with what can be found by screening the soil and rubble down below.

TOPANGA

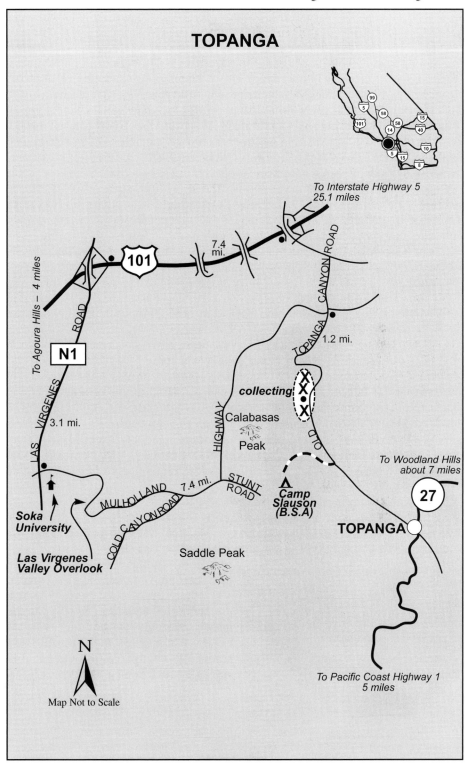

To Interstate Highway 5
25.1 miles

7.4 mi.

101

TOPANGA CANYON ROAD

1.2 mi.

To Agoura Hills – 4 miles

ROAD

N1

LAS VIRGENES

3.1 mi.

collecting

Calabasas
Peak

HIGHWAY

OLD

To Woodland Hills
about 7 miles

27

TOPANGA

MULHOLLAND

COLD CANYON ROAD

7.4 mi.

STUNT
ROAD

Camp
Slauson
(B.S.A)

Soka
University

Las Virgenes
Valley Overlook

Saddle Peak

N

Map Not to Scale

To Pacific Coast Highway 1
5 miles

ACTON

The region surrounding Acton offers a number of collecting possibilities. To access the four sites illustrated on the accompanying map, go northeast on State Highway 14 about 22 miles from where it meets Interstate Highway 5. At that point, take Crown Valley Road south 1.8 miles to Soledad Canyon Road. Turn left and proceed another 1.8 miles to Aliso Canyon Road, where you should then go right 2.7 more miles, then right again onto the well-graded gravel. Continue 3.3 miles, and then follow the tracks on the south, as they wind their way up the mountain another 2 miles to Site A. This spot is well-known for its pegmatite minerals, and numerous such outcrops can be seen throughout the area. Look along the road and in the surrounding hills, for quite a distance in all directions of the given mileage, for mica books, ilmenite and beautiful pink feldspar crystals.

Site B is reached by returning to the main road and climbing back to the upper ridge, past Perspiration Point, as shown on the map. The road is steep, but most rugged vehicles should have no problem. Look for more mica and ilmenite, in addition to actinolite, green schist and hornblende. These often showy minerals are found within the huge boulders situated alongside the road for quite a distance.

To get to Site C from Acton, go north from town on Crown Valley Road 0.4 miles to Escondido Canyon Road, where you should turn left. Continue 0.3 miles and bear left onto Hubbard Road. Drive past the house at the intersection and search the hill north of Hubbard Road for small pieces of banded agate, massive olivine and colorful jasper. Small quantities can also be found in the lowlands, but the best is picked up higher on the slopes.

Site D is centered around the now abandoned Emma Copper Mine. To get there, return to Acton and head southwest on Soledad Canyon Road about 2.2 miles. There on the right, high on the mountain, you will see what remains of the old mine.

Ruts lead from the pavement to where you must park at the base of the hill. From there, it is necessary to hike along the old road up to the dumps. Do not attempt driving that very steep and severely washed out road up the mountainside, even if you have a four-wheel drive vehicle.

On the dumps rockhounds can get nice specimens of malachite, chrysocolla and other copper ores, most of which are no more than a colorful stain on the native rock. As is the case with all mines, if it appears that the collecting status has changed, don't collect until you ascertain if there are any restrictions.

Examining a Specimen
Found at Site B

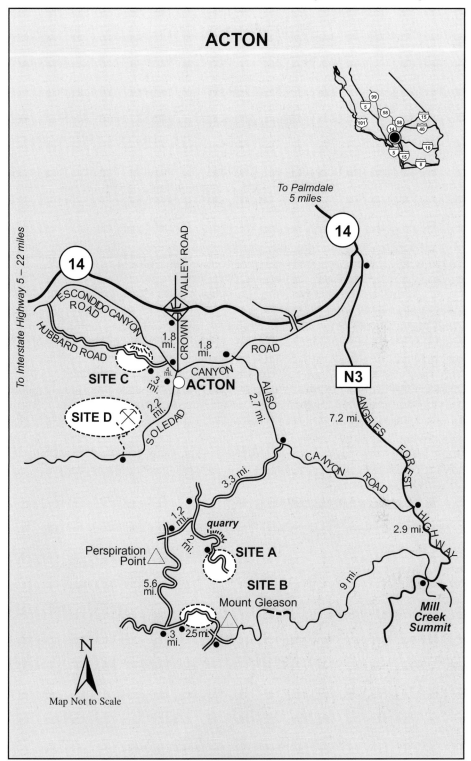

ACTON

To Palmdale
5 miles

14

To Interstate Highway 5 – 22 miles

14

CROWN VALLEY ROAD

ESCONDIDO CANYON ROAD

HUBBARD ROAD

1.8 mi.

1.8 mi.

ROAD

.4 mi.

CANYON

.3 mi.

SITE C

ACTON

SITE D

2.2 mi.

SOLEDAD

ALISO

2.7 mi.

N3

7.2 mi.

ANGELES FOREST HIGHWAY

CA NYON ROAD

3.3 mi.

2.9 mi.

1.2 mi.

.2 mi.

quarry

SITE A

Perspiration Point

SITE B

9 mi.

5.6 mi.

Mount Gleason

Mill Creek Summit

.3 mi.

2.5 mi.

N

Map Not to Scale

RINCON FOSSILS

This is a very convenient spot to find a variety of ancient marine fossils. The primary collecting site is on a highway offramp, making it most important to be careful. To get there, take U.S. Highway 101 west from Ventura, about 17 miles, to the State Highway 150 offramp. Just after leaving U.S. Highway 101, on the right is the fossil-filled bank. Pull well to the side of the wide offramp, less than 0.1 miles from the freeway. It is in that bank where you can find a lot of fossilized shells.

Much of what can be gathered there is just chips and pieces, but there are complete specimens, if you are willing to spend a little time doing some LIGHT digging. The white shells are easily spotted against the soft brown soil, helping to simplify the search.

When you examine what is left of these ancient inhabitants of the region, it is difficult to imagine that they are nearly one million years old. There is a considerable variety of shell types to be found here including snail shells, clam shells, sea worm tubes and countless other items.

If you feel uncomfortable collecting next to such a busy offramp, there are other less conspicuous places on the opposite side of the hill. To get there, continue to the stop sign at State Highway 150, about 0.1 miles farther. Turn right, go 0.5 miles to Rincon Hill Road, and turn right again. Most of the exposed banks along this stretch of road, continuing 0.8 miles back to U.S. Highway 101, provide collectors with the same type fossils as were found next to the offramp. Finding a good place to pull off the pavement, locating the fossil-bearing soil amongst the thick foliage, and ascertaining which portions of the hill are open to collectors and which are not makes it somewhat of a challenge.

If you are patient, and careful when walking on the roadways and climbing on the sometimes crumbly hillsides, you should be able to gather a good selection of million-year-old shells.

Searching for Fossils Along the Offramp

RINCON

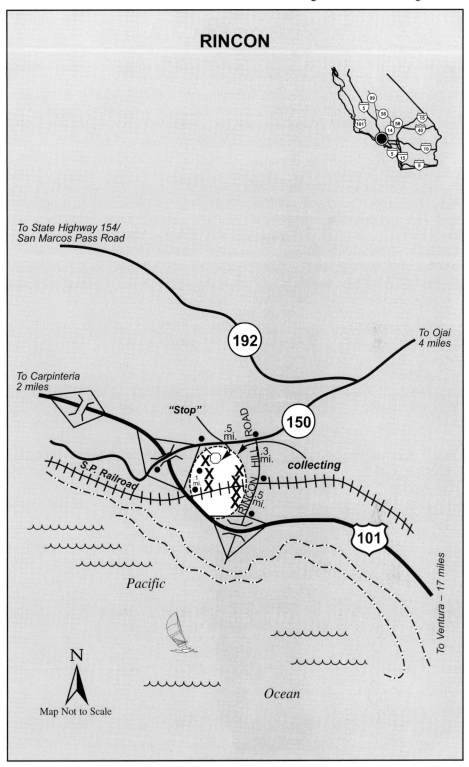

To State Highway 154/
San Marcos Pass Road

192

To Ojai
4 miles

To Carpinteria
2 miles

"Stop"

RINCON HILL ROAD

.5
mi.

150

.3
mi.

collecting

S.P. Railroad

.1
mi.

.5
mi.

101

To Ventura – 17 miles

Pacific

N

Map Not to Scale

Ocean

SANTA BARBARA FOSSILS

The two spots illustrated on the accompanying map can provide collectors with a variety of ancient marine fossils. To get to Site A, go west from Santa Barbara on U.S. Highway 101 about 4 miles to the State Highway 154 turnoff. After leaving U.S. Highway 101, instead of turning right onto State Highway 154, bear straight ahead on Calle Real for 0.9 miles. Turn right on the road to the dump, and after going only 0.1 miles, a small turnout will be seen and a little trail leading from it onto the ridge. That ridge and the lower roadcut comprise Site A.

One can gather a lot of very well-preserved scallop shells, as well as a variety of other shells representing the ancient sea life which inhabited this area so many years ago. There are a lot of chips and fragments, but if you carefully scrape into the somewhat soft soil, complete specimens can often be obtained. Occasionally, a nice one will be found amongst rubble below the roadcut, but such finds are rare. Digging is not well accepted here, so be discreet. Find loose specimens or partially exposed shells which you can carefully "remove" from the surrounding soil. Look also for little fossilized snail shells, some of which are very interesting.

Site B is reached by returning to State Highway 154, heading north 0.5 miles, and then proceeding west on Cathedral Oaks Road another 2 miles. From there, go right onto Old San Marcos Road and follow it 3.1 miles as it winds its way up into the mountains. At the given mileage, there is a pullout, on the left, and it is there where you should park. The view from this lofty location is spectacular, and even if there were no fossils, it would probably be worth the drive.

The collecting is done in the roadcuts at the given mileage, for about 0.1 miles in either direction. The fossils are about forty million years old and consist of oysters, clams and occasionally, turritella snail shells. The oysters are by far the most abundant of what can be found, and some are incredibly well preserved, especially when you consider how long they have been here. Look in the rubble below the roadcuts for specimens, as well as within the banks themselves.

Site B

SANTA BARBARA

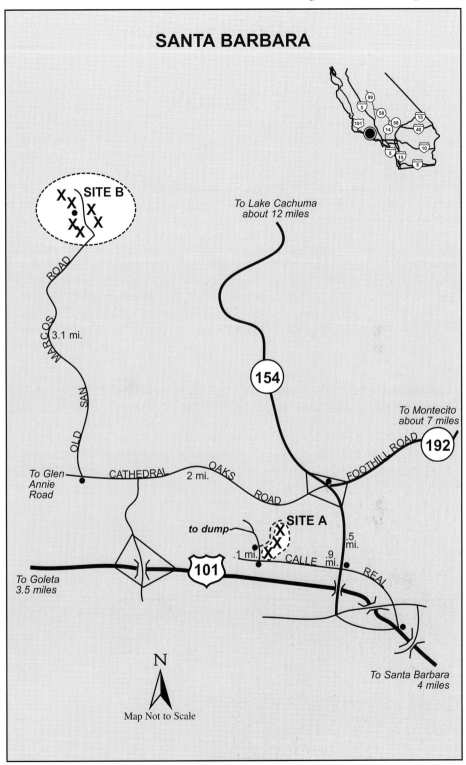

SITE B

To Lake Cachuma
about 12 miles

MARCOS ROAD

3.1 mi.

OLD SAN

154

To Montecito
about 7 miles

192

To Glen
Annie
Road

CATHEDRAL

OAKS

2 mi.

ROAD

FOOTHILL ROAD

to dump

SITE A

.5
mi.

.1 mi.

CALLE

.9.
mi.

REAL

101

To Goleta
3.5 miles

To Santa Barbara
4 miles

N

Map Not to Scale

CINCO CRYSTALS

Quartz and feldspar crystals can easily be found throughout the loose soil a few miles off State Highway 14, north of Mojave. To get to the rather condensed collecting area, go south 4.3 miles from where State Highway 14 intersects Redrock-Randsburg Road. Two homes can bee seen a short distance off the pavement, those indicating the turnoff. As you progress from the highway toward the mountains, do not enter the property fenced in by the homeowners. Jog around them, as shown, and then proceed up to prominent Sentinel Rock. That road is well-maintained, but very steep, so be certain your brakes are in good working order. In addition, do not attempt the drive in a motorhome or any underpowered vehicle. The trip to the summit afford numerous spectacular views of the desert, far below, providing an added bonus to trip.

Once you have gone 2.8 miles, bear right, going another 0.7 miles, and then pull off onto the tracks leading toward the base of the hill. Park at any convenient spot and hike up the jeep tracks to the north and east sides of prominent Sentinel Rock. Don't be tempted to drive up, since the soil is loose and it would be very easy to roll your vehicle. The hike is short and not too difficult.

The crystals can be found embedded in the large deposit of soft, clay-like material next to the ruts, and they are easily "popped" out with a small knife. The feldspar tends to be small but this is a great place to gather outstanding samples of unusual interlocking Carlsbad Twin crystallization. The quartz is often doubly-terminated, and some actually looks like little faceted diamonds. Those, too, are relatively small, usually measuring no more than half an inch in length. It doesn't take much time to gather a lot of nice feldspar and quartz crystals, since the entire ridge is loaded with them. Virtually every scoop of soil or piece of rock is filled with little gems. The quartz is less abundant and you must keep an eye out for it, since without close examination, it is possible to cast it aside as just more feldspar. Take a zip lock sandwich bag or something similar, in which to place your specimens.

The Road to the Cinco Collecting Area

CINCO

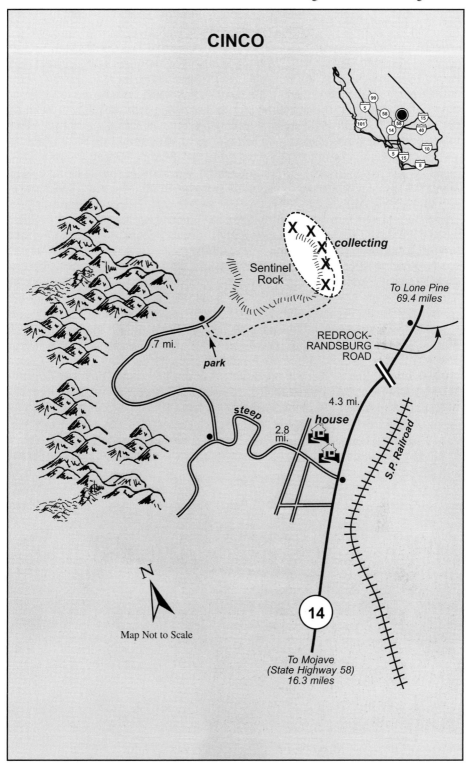

X X X
collecting
X
X
X
Sentinel
Rock
X

To Lone Pine
69.4 miles

.7 mi.

↑
park

REDROCK-
RANDSBURG
ROAD

4.3 mi.

steep

house

2.8
mi.

S.P. Railroad

N

Map Not to Scale

14

To Mojave
(State Highway 58)
16.3 miles

BROWN BUTTE

This location boasts petrified reeds, as well as nice agate, jasper and jasp-agate. To get there, go 7.9 miles east from Mojave on State Highway 58. At that point, turn south onto the dirt road and proceed 1.3 miles to the railroad crossing. The gate at this crossing is usually locked, but ruts can be seen on both sides of the gate where previous visitors have simply gone around. That is not suggested since it would be easy to get stuck attempting the maneuver, and if a train came through, the problem would become immense!

Best access, unless the gate is unlocked, is to park at the tracks and walk about 0.9 miles to the base of prominent Brown Butte. The most prolific area is immediately west of Brown Butte. There one can find good quality agate, jasp-agate, jasper and petrified reed, as well as occasional pieces of petrified wood. The deeply-colored chocolate brown jasper is especially desirable, and produces exquisite polished pieces.

Petrified reed is the prize at Brown Butte, and it offers unlimited cutting possibilities. Fascinating lapidary items can be made from this material depending upon how you cut it. Cutting perpendicular to the reed bundles creates the "eyes," while a parallel slice causes a series of lines.

There is a sufficient quantity of material available on the surface to satisfy most collectors, and each rain seems to expose more. If you have the energy better and more sizable chunks can be obtained by digging.

The hike to the primary collecting area is not bad, but remember that this is desert country. Be sure to take some water with you, as well as a sturdy collecting bag in which to haul back what you find.

It should also be noted that, due to the proximity of this site to Edwards Air Force Base and the Space Shuttle landing strip, some restrictions may be in effect regarding how far south from the railroad tracks you can go.

Road to Brown Butte

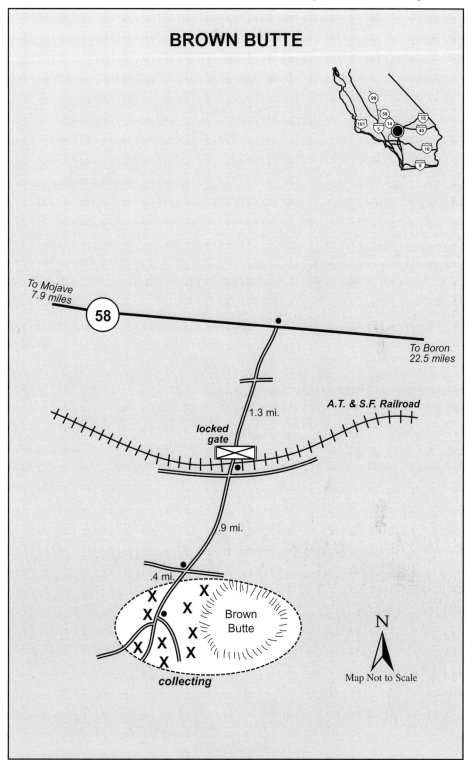

BROWN BUTTE

To Mojave
7.9 miles

58

To Boron
22.5 miles

1.3 mi.

A.T. & S.F. Railroad

locked
gate

.9 mi.

.4 mi.

X X
X X
X
X X X
X X

Brown
Butte

collecting

N

Map Not to Scale

ROSAMOND COLLECTIBLES

This location is centered around the well-known rockhounding landmark appropriately named Gem Hill, only a short distance north of the once booming Tropico Mine. Gem Hill is actually a series of adjacent knolls upon whose slopes one can find specimens of agate, jasper, rhyolite, common opal and petrified wood. Much of the rhyolite displays colorful bands, while the jasper and opal primarily are found in shades of green. The wood tends to be brown, with some regions of green and white. The most popular collectable at Gem Hill is the green moss and lace agate which can be found randomly scattered throughout the foothills. The surface material tends to be small, but more sizable pieces can be obtained by digging into areas of green hued soil.

To get to this well respected collecting locality, take the Rosamond Boulevard Exit from State Highway 14 and go west 3.2 miles. At that point, the Mojave-Tropico Road intersects and you should turn right (north) and proceed 4.1 miles to where some dirt tracks lead off to the left (west).

Follow those ruts up to a mile, stopping randomly along the way. You can generally find material all along this road or along any of the branches heading south (left) into the little hills. Since this is such an easily accessible and longtime favorite mineral collecting location, most of the surface material has been gathered long ago. It now takes luck and patience and the willingness to do some walking away from the easy access provided by the numerous roads and ruts in the area. Be patient and allow sufficient time and you surely will not be disappointed with Gem Hill and the vast region surrounding it.

While in the area be sure to allow enough time to visit the old town and mine at Tropico. It is 0.7 miles north from Rosamond Boulevard alongside Mojave-Tropico Road. Not only will you be able to get a much better understanding of the local history, especially in regard to minerals and mining, but you might even be able to get some other rock collecting ideas from the proprietors. Generally the mine is open for tours on weekends.

A View of Gem Hill

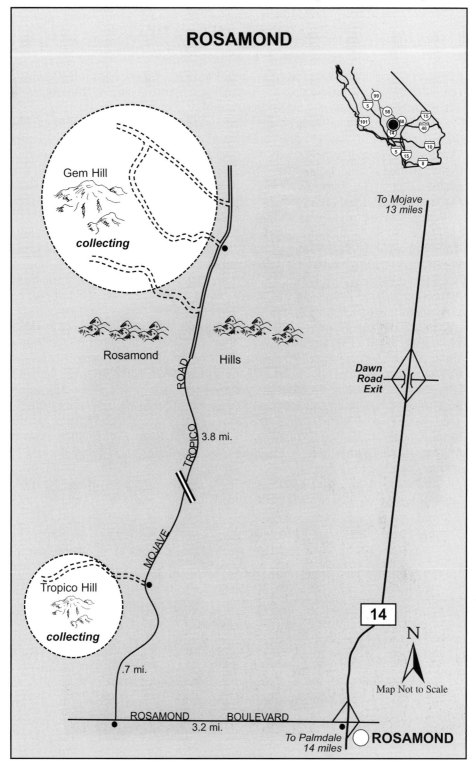

ROSAMOND

Gem Hill

collecting

Rosamond

Hills

ROAD

TROPICO

3.8 mi.

MOJAVE

Tropico Hill

collecting

.7 mi.

To Mojave
13 miles

**Dawn
Road
Exit**

14

N

Map Not to Scale

ROSAMOND   BOULEVARD
3.2 mi.

To Palmdale
14 miles

◯ **ROSAMOND**

LAKE CACHUMA

At one time, this location was closed in an effort to protect the endangered red-legged frog. That status appears to have changed and collecting is allowed again. If, however, when you visit, there are any indications the region is again closed, please obey posted regulations.

Good specimens of jasper, petrified wood and fossilized shells can be found in the region east of Lake Cachuma, in and around the Santa Ynez River. To get there, take State Highway 154 to Paradise Road, which is about 10.7 miles northwest of U.S. Highway 101. Turn east, as shown on the map, and go 3.4 miles to the White Rock Picnic Area, which is situated about 0.3 miles past the Paradise Campground. Park there and hike a few yards north to the primary collecting area.

Search for the jasper and wood in the riverbed, on its banks and throughout the hills on the opposite side. Usually, there is little or no water in the Santa Ynez River, making it relatively safe to ford, but not always! Use good judgment before crossing. If you can't see the bottom, regard it as unsafe and be content with what can be found on the south. Even if you can see the bottom, be careful since the rocks can be slick.

The jasper occurs in brightly-colored shades of orange and yellow, while the scarce wood is primarily brown. The shells are embedded in the easily spotted white limestone on the northern cliffs. To get to the finest specimens, it is necessary to remove chunks of the limestone directly from the hillside, using hard rock tools, such as sledgehammers, gads and chisels. The effort isn't too bad, especially if you are able to extract a few pieces containing a good sampling of well formed fossils. Once you get a good chunk of the fossil-bearing limestone, it is advisable to keep it until you get to a location where you can trim it with care. It takes some delicate and diligent work to scrape away the encasing host rock to best display the fossils.

If you want to spend some time in this pleasant location, the Paradise Campground would be a good place to consider.

Exploring the Area Around the Santa Ynez River

LAKE CACHUMA

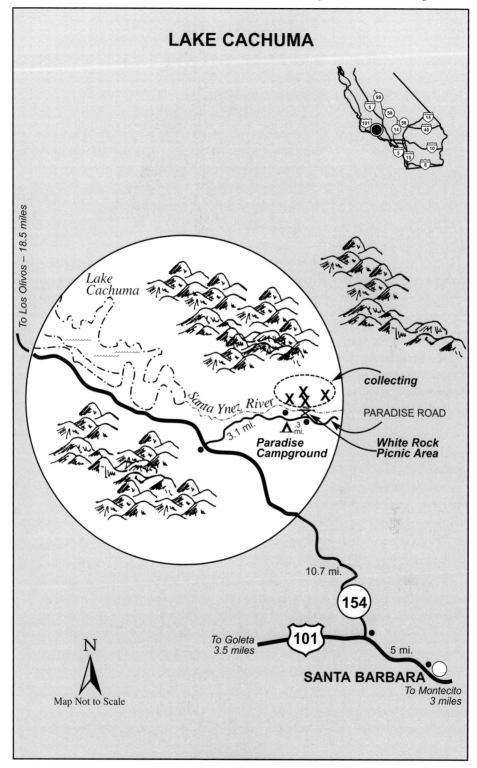

To Los Olivos – 18.5 miles

Lake Cachuma

Santa Ynez River

3.1 mi.

Paradise Campground

.3 mi.

collecting

PARADISE ROAD

White Rock Picnic Area

10.7 mi.

154

101

To Goleta 3.5 miles

5 mi.

SANTA BARBARA

To Montecito 3 miles

N

Map Not to Scale

LOS OLIVOS

Just about all of the roadcuts between Points A and B on the accompanying map provide collectors with a lot of nice green serpentine and soapstone. This is not a trip for motor homes, since there are many spots along the way where trees overhang the road, making it impossible for large vehicles to get through.

To get there, take State Highway 154 southeast from U.S. Highway 101 for 2.8 miles to Los Olivos. Go north on Figueroa Mountain Road 8.2 miles to the first of many soapstone-bearing roadcuts, this being designated as Point A, on the map. From that point, continuing at least another 11 miles to Point B, virtually every roadcut contains some soapstone (a green massive form of talc) and/or serpentine. Stop at any or all of them to sample what is available. Just be certain to pull well off the road, since people traveling through here will not be expecting to see stopped vehicles (or pedestrians). The road is paved, but full of curves, and is very narrow in places.

The best collecting along this stretch is the renowned Soapstone Hill, 5.9 miles east of Point A, and 1 mile past the Figueroa Campground turnoff. This remarkable little knoll is easy to spot and the slopes are covered with specimens ranging in size from pebbles to colossal boulders. Much of what can be found throughout the region is flaky, but there is still a remarkable amount of good solid material. That which displays little or no layering can be used for carving and other lapidary applications, while the other, if brightly colored, might still be nice for display. The hues range from gray to bright green, but most is olive green.

There is a fairly good spot to find some colorful chert and jasper about 0.4 miles past Soapstone Hill. Look on both sides of the road, throughout the trees, for good tumbling size specimens. Nothing is overly plentiful, but it might be worth the stop, while in the area.

There are a few nice Forest Service campgrounds within the Los Padres National Forest, and one in particular is very convenient, that being the Figueroa Campground, as shown on the map.

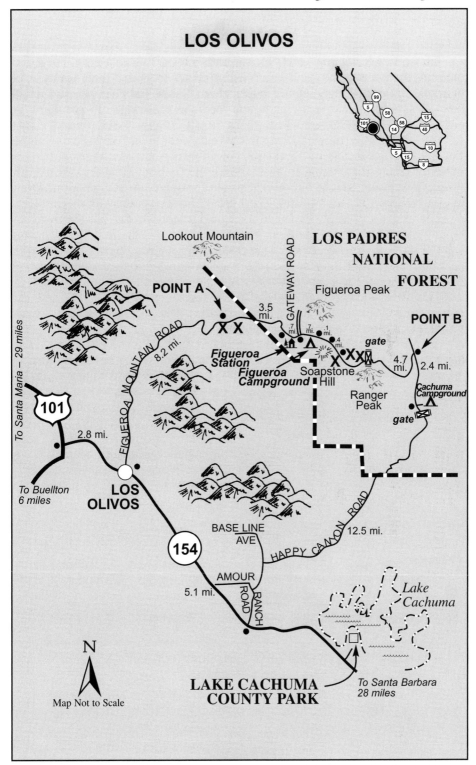

LOS OLIVOS

Lookout Mountain

LOS PADRES
NATIONAL
FOREST

GATEWAY ROAD

Figueroa Peak

POINT A

3.5
mi.

.7
mi.

.7
mi.

.1
mi.

.4
mi.

gate

POINT B

FIGUEROA MOUNTAIN ROAD

8.2 mi.

*Figueroa
Station*

*Figueroa
Campground*

Soapstone
Hill

Ranger
Peak

4.7
mi.

2.4 mi.

*Cachuma
Campground*

gate

To Santa Maria – 29 miles

101

2.8 mi.

*To Buellton
6 miles*

LOS
OLIVOS

154

BASE LINE
AVE

AMOUR

5.1 mi.

RANCH
ROAD

HAPPY CANYON ROAD

12.5 mi.

*Lake
Cachuma*

N

Map Not to Scale

LAKE CACHUMA
COUNTY PARK

*To Santa Barbara
28 miles*

JALAMA BEACH

Jalama Beach not only offers rockhounds a lot of fine collecting, but it also provides them a most scenic location within which to pursue their hobby. A lot of quality travertine onyx, agate, jasper, chert, fossils and even petrified whale bone can be found along the shoreline for quite a distance. To get there, go about 36 miles west from Santa Barbara on U.S. Highway 101, and then turn onto U.S. Highway 1 toward Lompoc. Drive an additional 13.7 miles to Jalama Road where you should turn west and continue another 14.7 miles to the park entrance. At time of publication, there was a $5 per day charge to use the county beach and $16 to $22 was required for overnight camping. For group reservations, call (805) 934-6211. There is a $25 reservation fee for this service.

The agate and jasper is found all along the beach, for quite a distance. Simply walk along the shorebreak as far as you care to go, in either direction, keeping an eye out for the easily spotted pebbles. Most occurs in shades of brown, honey, gold and clear, often displaying beautiful, lace-like patterns which can be used to make exquisite cabochons.

The travertine onyx emanates from a huge deposit which jets into the ocean about 1.5 miles north of the parking area. It is easy to see from the main beach, and you can't miss it while hiking.

A lot of the travertine is beautiful, being filled with colored bands. Most are solid and capable of taking a good polish. The best is gathered by directly attacking the deposit with hard rock tools, such as a sledgehammer, gads, pry bars and chisels.

Of course, that necessitates carrying all that equipment with you from the parking area, and hauling it and whatever you find all the way back. That does force collectors to be very selective. If that effort does not appeal to you, there are usually some onyx chunks and pebbles lying around the deposit, but, surprisingly, not a lot.

Fossils have been found throughout the cliffs just east of the beach, but be very careful if you do any digging there. Material from above is unstable, and it can be loosened easily. Look for fossil fish and plant imprints.

Picking up Specimens

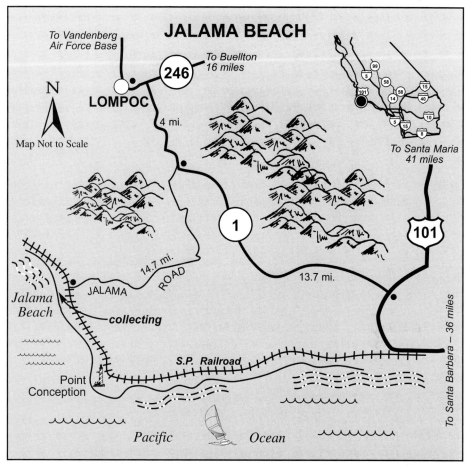

View of the Scenic Jalama Beach Collecting Area

SAN LUIS OBISPO

Nice little quartz crystals can be found scattered throughout the soil and within cavities of boulders in a scenic collecting location overlooking San Luis Obispo. To get there, take U.S. Highway 101 north from San Luis Obispo for 6 miles, and then turn left onto the paved road at Cuesta Summit. The turnoff comes up fast, and if you pass it, continue on to the Santa Margarita turnoff and double back. This is probably the safest approach, since traffic moves through here very fast and a left turn from such a highway is hazardous. From U.S. Highway 101, go up the winding mountain road 2.8 miles to the Botanical area, where you may want to spend a little time. From there, continue another 4 miles to the center of the collecting site, situated directly below the relay station.

The road leading up Cuesta Ridge is steep, narrow and winding, thereby not suitable for trailers or large motor homes. The journey does take you through some extremely scenic areas, as well as affording a number of breathtaking views.

At the given mileage, pull off the pavement and look carefully through any of the many rock slides. Some of the quartz crystals will be loose, while others can be found filling pockets and cavities in the rocks and boulders. Pay particularly close attention to areas with the conspicuous orange soil. You will need a sledgehammer, gads and chisels to break up any suspicious rocks, and a good pair of gloves and goggles are also advisable. Once you expose a crystal-bearing cavity, it is essential that you be very careful when trying to remove them.

If splitting boulders doesn't appeal to you, there is usually a lot to be found by raking through the soil, on either side of the road, or by doing some screening. A small hand rake is helpful for sifting through the rubble, as is a little trowel. Keep in mind, that this location is relatively well-known, and a lot of surface collecting has taken place over the years. It takes diligent work and patience to find the elusive crystals, but the effort is often worth it. Specimens measuring up to 2 inches in length have been found here, but most tend to be considerably smaller.

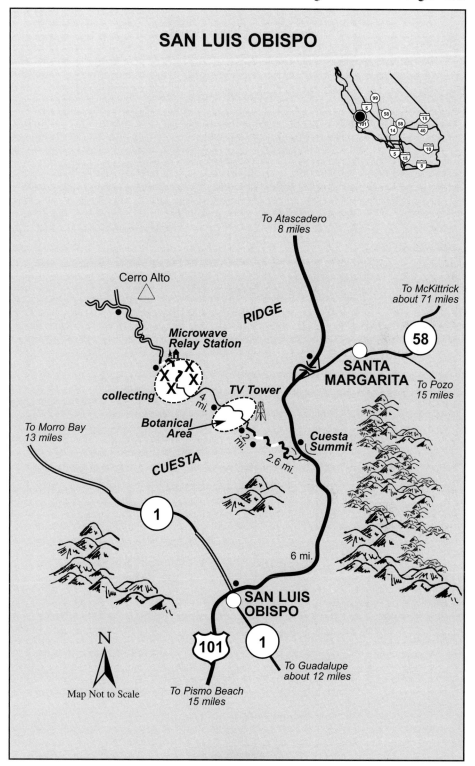

SAN LUIS OBISPO

To Atascadero
8 miles

Cerro Alto

To McKittrick
about 71 miles

RIDGE

58

Microwave
Relay Station

**SANTA
MARGARITA**

collecting

To Pozo
15 miles

TV Tower

4 mi.

*Botanical
Area*

2 mi.

*Cuesta
Summit*

To Morro Bay
13 miles

2.6 mi.

CUESTA

1

6 mi.

**SAN LUIS
OBISPO**

N

101

1

To Guadalupe
about 12 miles

Map Not to Scale

To Pismo Beach
15 miles

CAMBRIA MOONSTONE

The Pacific Ocean shoreline stretching from San Simeon and going south to Cambria is well-known for its good supply of eroded moonstone pebbles and occasional agates. In fact, a portion of the beach is actually named Moonstone Beach, to celebrate the little gemstones that can be found there.

There really isn't anything secret about getting the moonstone, which is an iridescent, faintly opal-like variety of feldspar. You simply access the beach anywhere between San Simeon and Cambria and start walking. The moonstones are not tough to find, appearing a little whitish pebbles. Just keep a keen eye to the ground as you walk and you surely will be able to gather a good number in a relatively short amount of time.

One easy access to the shoreline and potential collecting is to take Main Street from U.S. Highway 1 in Cambria to Moonstone Beach Road and then going north a far as you want. Park just about anywhere safe between there and San Simeon and explore the beach. One couldn't ask for a more relaxing and scenic place to pursue the hobby. In addition, the walking is flat and easy. The only problem is that collectors frequently hike along the water's edge much farther than they think they have and then proceed to lose track of where they parked their car. For that reason, try to identify a landmark and always be cognizant of your progress.

CAMBRIA

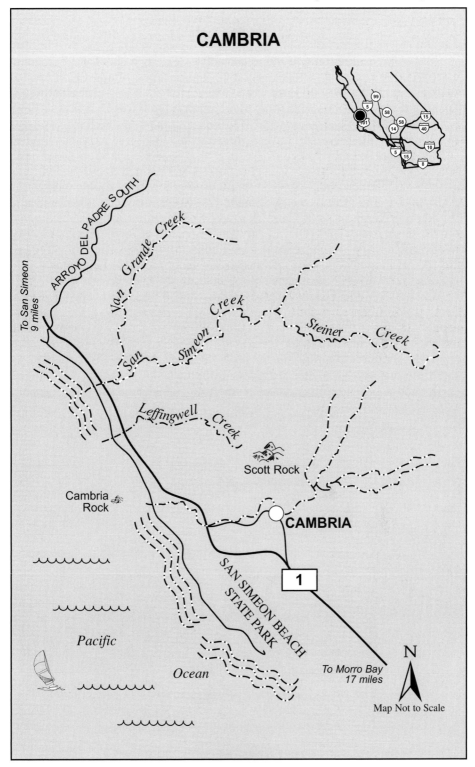

ARROYO DEL PADRE SOUTH

Van Grande Creek

San Simeon Creek

Steiner Creek

To San Simeon
9 miles

Leffingwell Creek

Scott Rock

Cambria
Rock

CAMBRIA

SAN SIMEON BEACH STATE PARK

1

Pacific

Ocean

To Morro Bay
17 miles

N

Map Not to Scale

DEVILS DEN

Fossilized shells can be found in a roadcut on both sides of the pavement, at the location shown on the accompanying map. To get there, take the 25th Avenue Exit from Interstate Highway 5, which is about 4 miles south of where State Highway 41 intersects. From there, simply go south 3.2 miles to the small roadcut which marks the site. If you pass it, just double back 2.6 miles from where Devils Den Road meets 25th Avenue.

It is imperative that you park well off the road while collecting here, since motorists will not be expecting to encounter a parked car. Shells and chunks of rock containing shells can be found throughout the rubble below the roadcut, and some very nice specimens can be procured by simply sorting through those regions. The finest are usually obtained by doing some digging into the bank itself. The rock and surrounding soil is relatively soft, so it isn't overly difficult. Try to remove as sizable a chunk of the fossil-bearing stone as you can. A hammer, pry bar, gads and/or chisels are most helpful, but care must be taken not to damage any of the delicate shells.

It is advisable to simply remove chunks of the fossil rock and then save them until you get to a place where you can more carefully work. The best display pieces are a result of many hours of patient removal of encasing soil and rock with a small knife or ice pick. If done properly, the resulting pieces are extremely interesting, worthy of display in any collection. This is especially true if the rock contains a lot of undamaged shells.

Do not knock anything onto the highway while working here, since it could be very hazardous to vehicles using this relatively well traveled stretch of road.

Parked Well Off the Road at the Collecting Area

DEVILS DEN

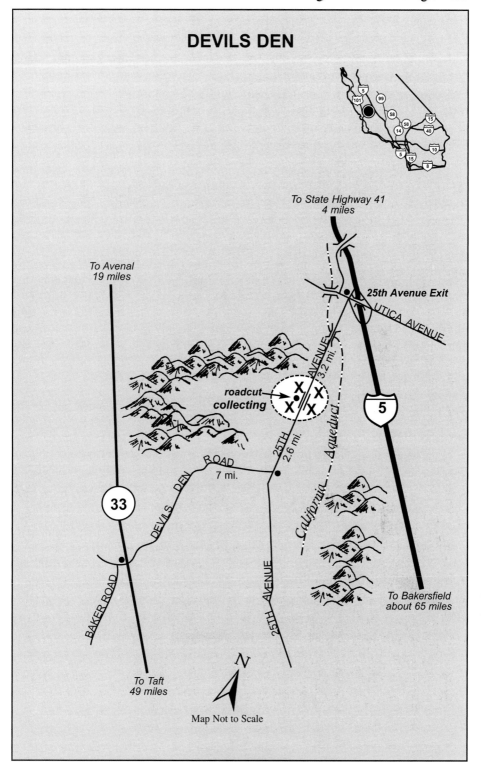

To State Highway 41
4 miles

To Avenal
19 miles

25th Avenue Exit

UTICA AVENUE

AVENUE 3.2 mi.

roadcut
collecting

X X
X X

5

25TH 2.6 mi.

DEVILS DEN ROAD
7 mi.

33

BAKER ROAD

25TH AVENUE

To Bakersfield
about 65 miles

California Aqueduct

To Taft
49 miles

N

Map Not to Scale

KETTLEMAN HILLS

One of the best fossil sites in California is within the Kettleman Hills, about 80 miles north of Bakersfield. It is VERY IMPORTANT to understand that this collecting site is on PRIVATE LAND and a collecting permit MUST be requested through Chevron Oil Company, well in advance of your trip. Please do not visit without first getting permission to do so. It would be a shame for some thoughtless collector to trespass and have the site completely closed.

To apply for a Permit of Entry, make your request, in writing, at least three weeks in advance, to: Chevron Company, 4900 California Avenue, P.O. Box 1392, Bakersfield, CA 93302. The primary collecting site lies in Section 35, Township 22 South, Range 17 East; and Section 1, Township 22 South, Range 17 East. That information, as well as the date(s) you will be there and how many people will accompany you, must be entered onto the permit by the Chevron Offices. If the date you request is available, the permit will be sent for a signature. Be advised that access is limited, and educational groups are given first priority. It should also be noted that there are no guarantees a permit will be granted, since there are many factors contributing to their issuance.

To get to the center of the site (if, and only if, you have a permit!), take the Lassen Avenue turnoff from Interstate Highway 5, as illustrated on the accompanying map. You first must go west and then double back over the bridge toward Lemoore. Turn south onto the dirt road, immediately after crossing the highway. Proceed south, paralleling Interstate Highway 5, 1.7 miles, then bear right at the fork another 0.5 miles. At that point, turn right, cross over the bridge and pass through the gate, continuing about 1.2 more miles. The dirt road is rough in places, but there should be no problems for rugged vehicles, if driven carefully.

The best collecting is north of the road, in and around the holes left by previous collectors. The list of what can be found here is lengthy, and includes sand dollars, scallops, coral, beaver and horse teeth, razor clams and a host of other marine and land fossils.

Another site is reached by driving west on State Highway 269 toward Avenal, about 3 miles, and then turning left to the Chevron Headquarters. From there, go south and explore any of the many nearby digging areas. As was the case at the first site, it is ESSENTIAL that you also request a permit to explore this region, and the procedure is the same.

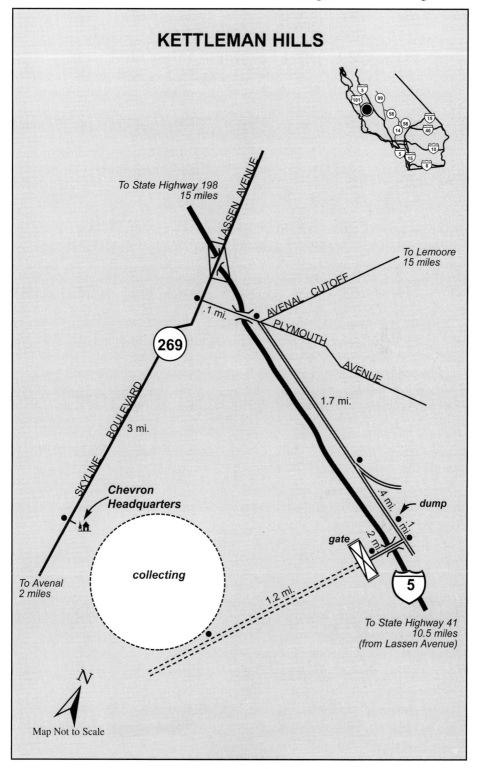

KETTLEMAN HILLS

To State Highway 198
15 miles

LASSEN AVENUE

To Lemoore
15 miles

AVENAL CUTOFF

PLYMOUTH

AVENUE

.1 mi.

269

1.7 mi.

SKYLINE BOULEVARD

3 mi.

**Chevron
Headquarters**

.4 mi.

dump

.1 mi.

To Avenal
2 miles

collecting

gate

.2 mi.

5

1.2 mi.

To State Highway 41
10.5 miles
(from Lassen Avenue)

N

Map Not to Scale

ANT HILL SHARK'S TEETH

At one time, Shark Tooth Hill just northeast of Bakersfield, was one of the best places in the entire country to find good quality shark's teeth, as well as many other types of fossils. Due to oil drilling and some unfortunate abuse of collecting privileges, that locality was closed years ago.

A very similar, but lesser known site, is situated a few miles farther south near beautiful Hart Park. To get to Ant Hill, the center of that collecting area, take State Highway 178 about 8.3 miles east from where it intersects State Highway 204 in Bakersfield. At that point, turn left on the Harrel Highway and go another 2.5 miles. There is a litter removal sign on the side of the road, just before the ruts upon which you should turn. Go left, then immediately right, and then left again through the gate. Proceed between the mountains, approximately 0.7 miles. An old metal bunker can be seen on the hillside to the left. Follow any of the ruts up to the base of the bunker and park near the concrete slabs. If you are not sure your vehicle can get there from the main road, park down below and hike the short distance.

The prime collecting area is easy to see, being situated on the hillside, above the bunker. There is a continuous, linear series of excavations along the somewhat thin, fossil-bearing strata made by previous collectors, which marks where you should start. The bone and teeth tend to be a little darker than the host soil.

Most collectors remove portions of the ancient fossil-bearing soil and then CAREFULLY break it up, while looking for the teeth and bone. A screen will help separate the soil, and can greatly enhance the quality of your search. Occasionally, some chunks are best left intact, since outstanding display pieces can be made from them, if they contain partially exposed shark's teeth and/or bone. Careful "cleaning" and further exposure with an ice pick and/or knife can greatly enhance such specimens.

Parked Near the Old Metal Bunker on the Hillside

ANT HILL

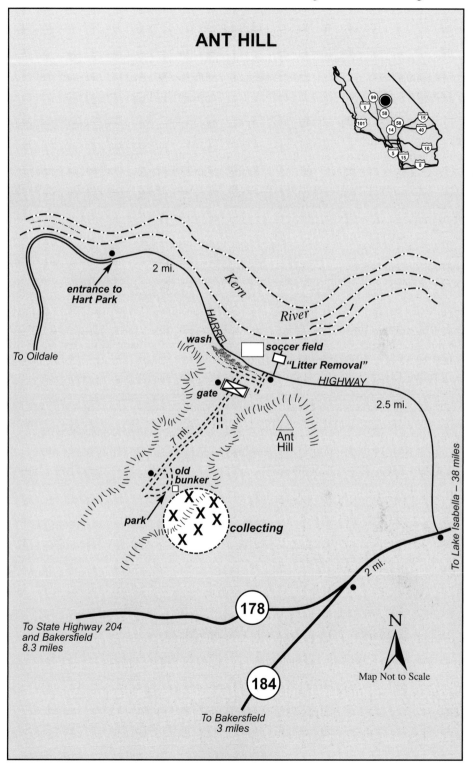

entrance to
Hart Park

2 mi.

Kern

River

To Oildale

HARREL

wash

soccer field

"Litter Removal"

HIGHWAY

gate

2.5 mi.

Ant
Hill

.7 mi.

old
bunker

park

X X X
X X X X
X X
X

collecting

To Lake Isabella – 38 miles

178

2 mi.

To State Highway 204
and Bakersfield
8.3 miles

N

Map Not to Scale

184

To Bakersfield
3 miles

COALINGA

These two sites feature petrified wood, chalcedony, fossil shells, chert, jasper and banded rhyolite, as well as some fascinating specimens of petrified coral. To get from Coalinga to Site A, take Jayne Avenue about 5 miles west from town, and go left onto Alpine Avenue, following State Highway 33. Drive another 2.5 miles, turn right onto Lost Hills Avenue, and continue 2.5 more miles to Jacalitos Creek Road, where you should turn left. From that intersection, continuing for quite a distance, good specimens can be found on both banks of Jacalitos Creek, just north of the road. The chert and jasper are generally quite colorful, and the rhyolite is a prize, due to its delicate banding. Chalcedony, petrified wood, coral and shells are rare, but are still worth looking for.

Be advised that much of Site A is on PRIVATE PROPERTY, and you should not trespass without first getting permission to do so. The collectibles are found amongst the river gravel and boulders on either side of the creek. If the water level is shallow, you may want to explore both sides. Be very cautious if you do choose to cross, though. The wet rock is often extremely slick, and it is easy to slip. There is plenty to be found on the south, but if you must explore the north and don't feel comfortable crossing through the water, walk back to Lost Hills Road and go over the bridge to the other side.

Site B is accessed by returning to State Highway 33 and going south 2.7 miles to where a faint dirt road will be seen heading off to the west, just before crossing Chino Creek. The material found here doesn't seem to be as plentiful as at Site A, but it does offer rockhounds the opportunity to gather additional jasper, wood, chalcedony, fossils and rhyolite. Be sure to walk a distance along to creek in order to gather a good variety of specimens. As was the case at Site A, there is private property throughout this location also. In addition, if the gate is locked shut, respect the rights of the property owners and do not go any farther.

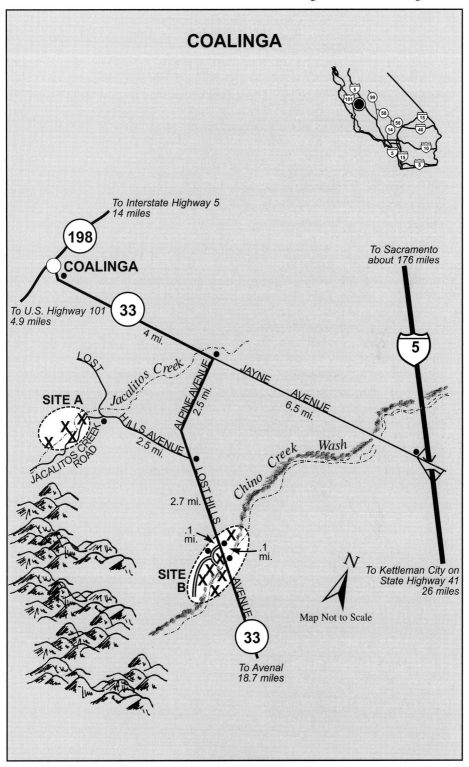

COALINGA

To Interstate Highway 5
14 miles

198

COALINGA

To Sacramento
about 176 miles

To U.S. Highway 101
4.9 miles

33

4 mi.

LOST

Jacalitos Creek

JAYNE AVENUE
6.5 mi.

ALPINE AVENUE
2.5 mi.

5

SITE A

HILLS AVENUE
2.5 mi.

X X
X X

JACALITOS CREEK ROAD

Chino Creek Wash

S. LOST HILLS AVENUE

2.7 mi.

.1 mi.

X
.1 mi.

SITE B

X X X
X

To Kettleman City on
State Highway 41
26 miles

N

Map Not to Scale

33

To Avenal
18.7 miles

CLEAR CREEK

This is a rockhound's paradise, boasting, among other things, tons of serpentine, jade, agate, cinnabar, quartz crystals, jadeite, chromite and green uvarovite garnet. There is so much available that it is often difficult to determine exactly what to keep and what to leave behind. When it seems you have found the "perfect" specimen, something better turns up.

To get to the Clear Creek collecting area, take State Highway 25 south from Hollister about 41 miles to Coalinga Road. Go east on Coalinga Road for 16 miles to Clear Creek Road, which is just beyond the Hernandez Reservoir. If you have time, there are many roadcuts along this stretch which contain good quality, green serpentine, and a few stops might prove to be fruitful. If you do explore any of the little roadcuts, be sure to pull well off the pavement.

To get to the primary site, turn left onto Clear Creek Road and go about 2.3 miles to the Clear Creek Land Management Area boundary. Even though you will see a lot of nice green jadeite and serpentine along this stretch of road, it is primarily on private property, making it necessary to wait until entering public lands before gathering anything. It should be also mentioned that Clear Creek Road crosses the creek a number of times. That will normally not present a problem to rugged vehicles, but whether you attempt crossing is completely up to you. DO NOT ford the creek if it appears flooded or if you have any doubts.

Once inside the public area, bright green rocks will be seen, scattered just about everywhere. You will be tempted to immediately stop and start collecting. It is suggested that you drive all the way to Staging Area Five, about 6 miles from where Clear Creek Road intersected Coalinga Road, just to get an idea as to where the best deposits seem to be located.

To extract specimens from the primary deposits within the mountainside, or from large boulders, hard rock tools will be needed. Be sure to wear goggles, since just about all the minerals found here splinter when struck.

There are a few private claims in the Clear Creek region, but most are farther into the mountains, off the main road. Do not trespass.

Searching for Rocks and Minerals Along the Banks of Clear Creek

CLEAR CREEK

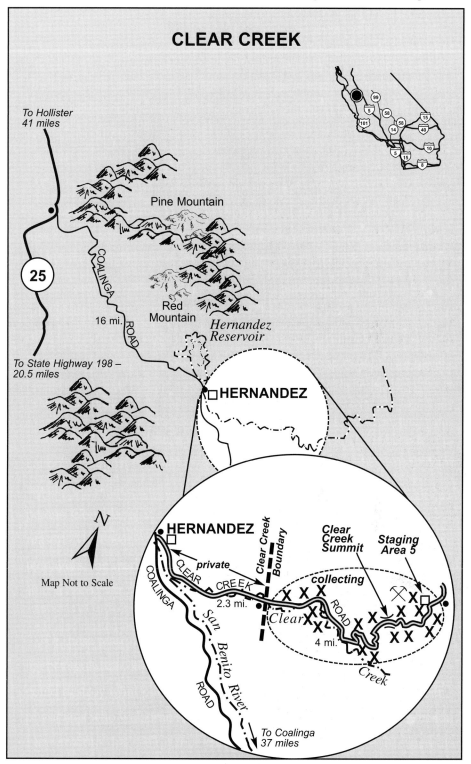

JUNNILA CLAIMS

This is a fee location which in recent years has been inconsistent in regard to allowing amateur collecting to take place on any of its properties. It is presented here as a supplement to the Clear Creek Site, and if open at the time you visit, it will simply make your visit all the more productive. The Junnila Claims, better known as Jade Mill, offers collectors an incredible amount of top quality jade, banded agate, plasma agate, magnesite, serpentine, cinnabar, zaratite, garnet, chrome ores, natrolite, Thomsonite crystals, datolite crystals, zoisite and countless other less abundant minerals. The charge to gather mineral specimens has been $10 per day, but that fee is subject to change.

Maps to the different Jade Mill claims will be provided upon payment of the collecting fee. Jade Mill's address is 4201 Clear Creek Road, and it is reached by following Clear Creek Road about 2.3 miles from the pavement to where a road marked with sign "4201" leads left, as shown on the accompanying map.

The rockhound claims lie throughout the Clear Creek region but are not situated along the main road. All are at least 5 miles from the main mine and a rugged, high-clearance vehicle is needed to get to most and four-wheel drive is highly desirable, even essential for access to some. Do not, under any circumstances, drive into areas your vehicle was not designed to go. This is a remote locality, and it would be extremely expensive to be towed out.

Samples of what can be found at the various claims can be viewed at Jade Mill, and it is highly recommended that you allow some time to carefully inspect them. That way, when in the field collecting, you will know exactly what to look for. The specimens on display at Jade Mill can only be sold wholesale, but just seeing them will definitely help to make your expedition more fruitful. In fact, seeing what is available at each of the different claims, might help you to decide which you want to visit.

Within the Clear Creek Management Area, there are a number of camp-grounds. A fire permit is required throughout the year. This is a beautiful spot in which to spend some time, and the minerals simply help to enhance that desirability.

Landscape View of the Collecting Area

JUNNILA CLAIMS

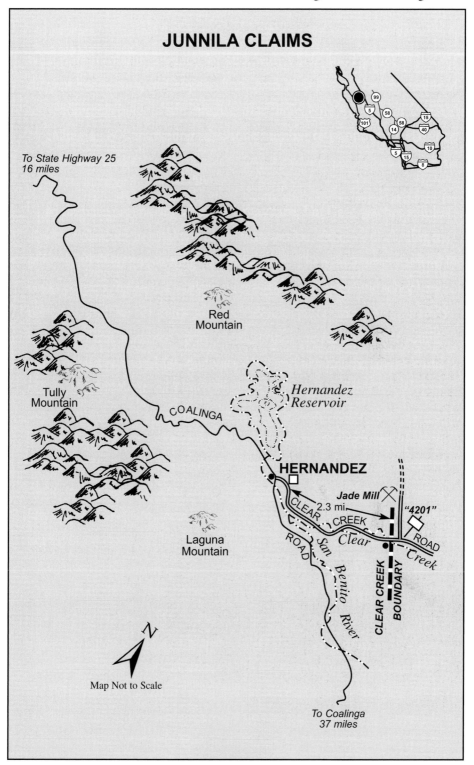

To State Highway 25
16 miles

Red
Mountain

Tully
Mountain

*Hernandez
Reservoir*

COALINGA

HERNANDEZ

Jade Mill

2.3 mi

CLEAR   CREEK

Clear

Creek

"4201"

ROAD

Laguna
Mountain

ROAD

San Benito River

CLEAR CREEK BOUNDARY

N

Map Not to Scale

To Coalinga
37 miles

GOVERNMENT AGENCIES

**ANZA BORREGO DESERT
STATE PARK**
200 Palm Canyon Drive
Borrego Springs, CA 92004
(619) 767-4684

BUREAU OF LAND MANAGEMENT
Street: 1620 L Street NW
Washington, DC 20036
Mailing: 1849 C Street NW
Washington, DC 20240
www.blm.gov

BLM BARSTOW FIELD OFFICE
2601 Barstow Road
Barstow, CA 92311
(760) 252-6000
http://www.ca.blm.gov/barstow/

BLM BISHOP FIELD OFFICE
785 North Main Street, Suite E
Bishop, CA 93514
(760) 872-4881
http://www.ca.blm.gov/bishop/

BLM BAKERSFIELD FIELD OFFICE
3801 Pegasus Drive
Bakersfield, CA 93308
(661) 391-6000
http://www.ca.blm.gov/bakersfield/

BLM CALIFORNIA DESERT DISTRICT
6221 Box Springs Boulevard
Riverside, CA 92507
(909) 697-5200
http://www.ca.blm.gov/cdd/

BLM EL CENTRO FIELD OFFICE
1661 South Fourth Street
El Centro, CA 92243
(760) 337-4400
http://www.ca.blm.gov/elcentro/

BLM NEEDLES FIELD OFFICE
707 West Broadway
Needles, CA 92363
(760) 326-6322
http://www.ca.blm.gov/needles/

**BLM PALM SPRINGS
FIELD OFFICE**
690 West Garnet Avenue
P.O. Box 581260
North Palm Springs, CA 92258
(760) 251-4800
http://www.ca.blm.gov/palmsprings/

**BLM RIDGECREST
FIELD OFFICE**
300 South Richmond Road
Ridgecrest, CA 93555
(760) 384-5400
http://www.ca.blm.gov/ridgecrest/

CALIFORNIA BLM STATE OFFICE
2800 Cottage Way, Suite W-1834
Sacramento, CA 95825-1886
(916) 978-4400
www.ca.blm.gov

**CALIFORNIA DEPARTMENT OF
CONSERVATION: CALIFORNIA
GEOLOGICAL SURVEY**
801 K Street, MS 24-01
Sacramento, CA 95814
(916) 322-1080
dmglib@consrv.ca.gov
www.consrv.ca.gov/dmg

**CANNELL MEADOW
RANGER DISTRICT**
105 Whitney Road
Kernville, CA 93238
(760) 376-3781

DEATH VALLEY NATIONAL PARK
P.O. Box 579
Death Valley, CA 92328
(760) 786-2331

INYO NATIONAL FOREST
873 North Main Street
Bishop, CA 93514
(760) 367-5500

JOSHUA TREE NATIONAL PARK
74485 National Park Drive
Twentynine Palms, CA 92277
(760) 367-7511

MOJAVE DESERT INFORMATION
P.O. Box 241
Baker, CA 92309
(760) 733-4040

MOJAVE NATIONAL PRESERVE
222 East Main Street, Suite 202
Barstow, CA 92311
(760) 255-8800

USDA FOREST SERVICE
1400 Independence Avenue SW
Washington, DC 20250
(202) 720-USDA

US GEOLOGICAL SURVEY
(888) ASK-USGS (275-8747)
www.usgs.gov

**US GEOLOGICAL SURVEY
    WESTERN REGION**
345 Middlefield Road
Menlo Park, CA 94025
(650) 853-8300

**US GEOLOGICAL SURVEY
    CENTRAL REGION**
205 6th and Kipling
Building #53
Entrance S1DFC
Denver, CO 80225
(303) 236-5900

**CALIFORNIA GEOLOGICAL
    SURVEY**
Placer Hall
6000 J Street
Sacramento, CA 95819-6129
(916) 278-3000
dc_ca@usgs.gov

GEM AND MINERAL SOCIETIES

The following gem and mineral societies meet regularly and provide a number of resources for the mineral collector gathering specimens in Southern California. At the time of publication, every effort was made to provide current contact information.

AMERICAN OPAL SOCIETY, INC.
P.O. Box 4875
Garden Grove, CA 92842-4875

SEARCHER GEM &
MINERAL SOCIETY
P.O. Box 3492
Anaheim, CA 92803

HI DESERT GOLD DIGGER
20162 Highway 18 #G-178
Apple Valley, CA 92307

KERN COUNTY MINERAL SOCIETY
P.O. Box 3004
Bakersfield, CA 93385-3004

MOJAVE DESERT GEM &
MINERAL SOCIETY
P.O. Box 138
Barstow, CA 92311

MOJAVE MINERALOGICAL SOCIETY
P.O. Box 511
Boron, CA 93596

SHADOW MOUNTAIN GEM &
MINERAL SOCIETY
P.O. Box 358
Cathedral City, CA 92234

INDIAN WELLS GEM &
MINERAL SOCIETY
P.O. Box 1481
China Lake, CA 93555

CONEJO GEM & MINERAL CLUB
P.O. Box 723
Newbury Park, CA 91319

ORANGE COAST MINERAL &
LAPIDARY SOCIETY
P.O. Box 10175
Costa Mesa, CA 92626

CULVER CITY ROCK &
MINERAL CLUB
P.O. Box 3324
Culver City, CA 90231

DELVERS GEM &
MINERAL SOCIETY
P.O. Box 4115
Downey, CA 90241

EL CAJON VALLEY GEM &
MINERAL SOCIETY
P.O. Box 451
El Cajon, CA 92022

ISLANDERS GEM &
MINERAL SOCIETY
P.O. Box 21007
El Cajon, CA 92021

NORTH ISLAND GEM &
MINERAL SOCIETY
P.O. Box 20772
El Cajon, CA 92021

IMPERIAL VALLEY GEM &
MINERAL SOCIETY
P.O. Box 1721
El Centro, CA 92244

SAN DIEGUITO GEM &
MINERAL CLUB
P.O. Box 2300863
Encinitas, CA 92024

PALOMAR GEM &
   MINERAL CLUB
P.O. Box 1583
Escondido, CA 92033

FALLBROOK GEM AND
   MINERAL SOCIETY
P.O. Box 62
Fallbrook, CA 92088

KAISER ROCK & GEM CLUB
9398 Live Oak
Fontana, CA 92335

WEST END PROSPECTORS
P.O. Box 834
Fontana, CA 92335

FACETERS' GUILD OF
   SOUTHERN CALIFORNIA
P.O. Box 8890-436
Fountain Valley, CA 92708

GLENDORA GEMS
859 E. Sierra Avenue
Glendora, CA 91740

NORTHROP GRUMANN GEM
   & MINERAL CLUB
1 Northrop Avenue
Hawthorne, CA 90250

SPORTSMAN'S CLUB OF
   JOSHUA TREE
P.O. Box 880
Joshua Tree, CA 92252

FOOTHILL GEM & MINERAL SOCIETY
6265 Altura Avenue
La Crescenta, CA 91214

NORTH ORANGE COUNTY
   GEM AND MINERAL SOCIETY
P.O. Box 653
La Habra, CA 90633

LA PUENTE GEM &
   MINERAL CLUB
P.O. Box 647
La Puente, CA 91744

LAKE ELSINORE GEM &
   MINERAL SOCIETY
33040 Dowman
Lake Elsinore, CA 92530

ANTELOPE VALLEY GEM
   & MINERAL CLUB
P.O. Box 69
Lancaster, CA 93584

VALLEY GEMS
9050 1/2 West Avenue J
Lancaster, CA 93536

PALOS VERDES GEM &
   MINERAL SOCIETY
P.O. Box 686
Lomita, CA 90717

LONG BEACH MINERAL &
   GEM SOCIETY
P.O. Box 4082
Long Beach, CA 90804

MINERAL RESEARCH SOCIETY
   OF SOUTHERN CALIFORNIA
4759 Blackthorne Avenue
Long Beach, CA 90808

SOUTHERN CALIFORNIA
   MICROMINERALOGISTS
609 West 36th Street
Long Beach, CA 90806

CENTINELA VALLEY GEM &
   MINERAL CLUB
5316 West 82nd Street
Los Angeles, CA 90045

LOS ANGELES LAPIDARY SOCIETY
2517 Federal Avenue
Los Angeles, CA 90064

LOS ANGELES
    MINERALOGICAL SOCIETY
228 South Oxford Avenue
Los Angeles, CA 90004

WEST LOS ANGELES JAPANESE
    AMERICAN LEAGUE
1928 Armacost Avenue
Los Angeles, CA 90025

SOUTHERN CALIFORNIA
    PALEONTOLOGICAL SOCIETY
1826 9th Street
Manhattan Beach, CA 90266

WESTSIDE MINERALOGISTS
1826 9th Street
Manhattan Beach, CA 90266

ORANGE COUNTY 49ERS
P.O. Box 781
Midway City, CA 92655

MONROVIA ROCKHOUNDS INC.
P.O. Box 553
Monrovia, CA 91016

MONTEREY PARK GEM SOCIETY
902 S. Garfield Avenue
Monterey Park, CA 91750

GLENDALE VERDUGO GEM &
    MINERAL SOCIETY
P.O. Box 265
Montrose, CA 91021

SAN FERNANDO VALLEY
    MINERAL & GEM SOCIETY
6300 Carlina Avenue
North Hollywood, CA 91606

NEEDLES GEM & MINERAL CLUB
251 Mustang Lane
Needles, CA 92365

SIERRA PELONA ROCK CLUB
P.O. Box 221256
Newhall, CA 91322

OXNARD GEM & MINERAL SOCIETY
P.O. Box 246
Oxnard, CA 93032

PALMDALE GEM &
    MINERAL CLUB
P.O. Box 900279
Palmdale, CA 93590

MINERALOGICAL SOCIETY OF
    SOUTHERN CALIFORNIA
P.O. Box 41027
Pasadena, CA 91114-8027

PASADENA LAPIDARY SOCIETY
P.O. Box 5025
Pasadena, CA 91117

POMONA ROCKHOUNDS
P.O. Box 494
Pomona, CA 91769

PORTERVILLE AREA GEM &
    MINERAL SOCIETY
10 Olive Drive
Porterville, CA 93257

SHASTA GEM & MINERAL
    SOCIETY, INC.
P.O. Box 424
Redding, CA 96099

RIVERSIDE TREASURE HUNTERS
P.O. Box 9647
Riverside, CA 92502

GEM CARVERS GUILD
197 South 1 Street
San Bernardino, CA 92410-2349

ORANGE BELT
    MINERALOGICAL SOCIETY
P.O. Box 5642
San Bernardino, CA 92412

VALLEY PROSPECTORS
P.O. Box 2923
San Bernardino, CA 92406

CAPISTRANO VALLEY ROCK &
MINERAL CLUB
P.O. Box 279
San Clemente, CA 92674

CONVAIR ROCKHOUNDS CLUB
10431 Baywood Avenue
San Diego, California 92126-3324

GEMOLOGICAL SOCIETY
OF SAN DIEGO
P.O. Box 16414
San Diego, CA 92176

SAN DIEGO LAPIDARY SOCIETY
5654 Mildred Street
San Diego, CA 92126

SAN DIEGO MINERAL AND
    GEM SOCIETY
1700 Village Place
San Diego, CA 92101

SAN LUIS OBISPO GEM &
    MINERAL CLUB
P.O. Box 563
San Luis Obispo, CA 93406

RANCHO SANTA MARGARITA
    GEM & MINERAL SOCIETY
P.O. Box 355
San Luis Rey, CA 92068

SANTA ANA ROCK AND
    MINERAL CLUB
P.O. Box 51
Santa Ana, CA 92702

SANTA BARBARA MINERAL
    AND GEM SOCIETY
P.O. Box 815
Santa Barbara, CA 93102

ORCUTT MINERAL SOCIETY INC.
P. O. Box 106
Santa Maria, CA. 93456

SANTA MONICA
    GEMOLOGICAL SOCIETY
P.O. Box 652
Santa Monica, CA 90404

VIP GEM & MINERAL SOCIETY
3108 San Angela Avenue
Simi Valley, CA 93063

TEHACHAPI VALLEY GEM AND
    MINERAL SOCIETY
P.O. Box 4400-132
Tehachapi, CA 93561

SOUTH BAY LAPIDARY AND
    MINERAL SOCIETY
P.O. Box 1606
Torrance, CA 90505

VENTURA GEM &
    MINERAL SOCIETY
P.O. Box 1573
Ventura, CA 93002

VICTOR VALLEY GEM &
    MINERAL CLUB
15056B 7th Street
Victorville, CA 92307

TULE GEM & MINERAL SOCIETY
P.O. Box 1061
Visalia, CA 93279

VISTA GEM & MINERAL SOCIETY
P.O. Box 1641
Vista, CA 92085-1641

**ROCKATOMICS GEM &
    MINERAL SOCIETY**
8500 Fallbrook
West Hills, CA 91305

**WHITTIER GEM &
    MINERAL SOCIETY**
P.O. Box 865
Whittier, CA 90608

**WOODLAND HILLS
    ROCK CHIPPERS**
P.O. Box 205
Woodland Hills, CA 91365

**YUCAIPA VALLEY GEM AND
    MINERAL SOCIETY**
P.O. Box 494
Yucaipa, CA 92399

MUSEUMS

The following museums are listed below to enhance your rockhounding trip throughout California.

**CALIFORNIA STATE MINING
AND MINERAL MUSEUM**
California State Parks
P. O. Box 1192
Mariposa, CA 95338
(209) 742-7625

**CALIFORNIA INSTITUTE OF
TECHNOLOGY**
Division of Geology and
Planetary Science
1201 East California Boulevard
Pasadena, CA 91125
(626) 395-6123

CATALINA ISLAND MUSEUM
P.O. Box 366
Avalon, CA 90704
(310) 510-2414
museum@catalinas.net
http://www.catalina.com/museum/html

**CHAPMAN'S GEM & MINERAL
SHOP AND MUSEUM**
4 Miles South on Highway 101
Fortuna CA 95540
(707) 725-4732
www.caohwy.com/c/chgemsmu.htm

**CHAW'SE INDIAN GRINDING
ROCK MUSEUM**
14881 Pine Grove/Volcano Road
Pine Grove, CA
(209) 296-7488
http://www.amadornet.net/travelers/
museums/chaw_se.html

**THE CHILDREN'S MUSEUM AT
LA HABRA**
301 South Euclid Street
La Habra, CA 90631
(562) 905-9693
http://www.lhcm.org/index.html

EXPLORATORIUM
3601 Lyon Street
San Francisco, CA 94123
(415) EXP-LORE
http://www.exploratorium.edu/

**GREAT VALLEY MUSEUM OF
NATURAL HISTORY**
1100 Stoddard Avenue
Modesto, CA 95350
(209) 575-6196
gvm@trex.cc-infonet.edu
http://mjc.yosemite.cc.ca.us/greatvalley/

**JURUPA MOUNTAINS
CULTURAL CENTER**
7621 Granite Hill Drive
Riverside, CA 92509
(909) 685-5818
admin@the-jmcc.org
http://www.the-jmcc.org/

KERN COUNTY MUSEUM
3801 Chester Avenue
Bakersfield, CA 93301
(661) 324-4052
http://www.kcMuseum.org/

**L.A. COUNTY MUSEUM OF
NATURAL HISTORY**
Mineral Sciences Section
900 Exposition Boulevard
Los Angeles, CA 90007
(213) 763-DINO
info@nhm.org
http://www.lam.mus.ca.us/minsci/

MATURANGO MUSEUM
100 East Las Flores Avenue
Ridgecrest, CA 93555
(760) 375-6900
http://www.maturango.org

MOJAVE RIVER VALLEY MUSEUM
270 East Virginia Way
Barstow, CA 92311
(760) 256-5452
http://mvm.4t.com/

NATURAL HISTORY MUSEUM OF LOS ANGELES COUNTY
900 Exposition Boulevard
Los Angeles, CA 90007
(213) 763-DINO
http://www.nhm.org/

PALM SPRINGS DESERT MUSEUM
101 Museum Drive
Palm Springs, CA 92262
(760) 325-0189
http://www.psmuseum.org/
info@psmuseum.org

PAGE MUSEUM/LA BREA TAR PITS
5801 Wilshire Boulevard
Los Angeles, CA 90036
(323) 934-PAGE
info@tarpits.org
http://www.tarpits.org/

SANTA BARBARA MUSEUM OF NATURAL HISTORY
2559 Puesta del Sol Road
Santa Barbara, CA 93105
(805) 682-4711
http://www.sbnature.org/

SAN BERNARDINO COUNTY MUSEUM
2024 Orange Tree Lane
Redlands, CA 92374-4560
(909) 307-2669/(888) BIRD-EGG
http://www.co.san-bernardino.ca.us/museum/

SAN DIEGO NATURAL HISTORY MUSEUM
1788 El Prado
Balboa Park
San Diego, CA 92101
(619) 232-3821
http://www.sdnhm.org/

UNIVERSITY OF CALIFORNIA BERKELEY MUSEUM OF PALEONTOLOGY
1101 Valley Life Sciences Building
Berkeley, CA 94720-4780
(510) 642-1821
http://www.ucmp.berkeley.edu/

UNIVERSITY OF CALIFORNIA LOS ANGELES
Department Earth and
    Space Sciences
595 Charles Young Drive East
3806 Geology Building
Box 951567
Los Angeles, CA 90095-1567
http://www.ess.ucla.edu/

VICTOR VALLEY MUSEUM
11873 Apple Valley Road
Apple Valley, CA 92308
(760) 240-2111
vvmmason@gte.net
http://www.vvmuseum.com/

WORLD MUSEUM OF NATURAL HISTORY
La Sierra University
4700 Pierce Street
Riverside, CA 92515
(909) 785-2209
http://www.lasierra.edu/centers/wmnh/
WMNH@lasierra.edu

MINERAL LOCATOR INDEX

GLOSSARY

A

ACTINOLITE — A dark-colored, often greenish amphibole, commonly found in schists and marbles.

AGATE — A banded, fine-grained or variegated chalcedony having its colors arranged in stripes, blended in clouds or showing moss-like forms.

AMETHYST — A purple or violet variety of quartz or corundum.

AMMONITE — Any of the flat, usually coiled fossil shells of the extinct order (Ammonoidea) of cephalopod mollusks dominant in the Mesozoic era.

APATITE — Variously colored, hard, hexagonal calcium minerals found mainly in sedimentary rocks, especially phosphate rock.

ARROYO — A dry gully, rivulet or stream.

ARSENIC — A metallic element of a steel-gray color and brilliant luster, and quite brittle. It forms alloys with most of the metals. Combined with sulfur, it forms orpiment and realgar, which are red and yellow sulphids of arsenic. Found in ore veins in crystalline rocks.

AZURITE — Brilliantly blue or violet monoclinic mineral that is an ore of copper.

B

BANDED AGATE — Agates with colors usually arranged in delicate parallel alternating bands or stripes of varying thickness. The bands are sometimes straight but usually wavy and concentric.

BARITE — A native form of barium sulphate of high specific gravity, occurring usually in colorless orthorhombic and tabular crystals.

BASALT — The most common extrusive igneous rock or lava. Basalt is primarily composed or pyroxene and feldspar. Highly fluid basalt that quickly covers a large area is referred to as flood basalt.

BED — The smallest layer of sedimentary rock, usually a layer from one depositional event such as a flood.

BERM — The margin or shoulder of a road, adjacent to and outside the paved or graded portion.

BLOODSTONE — A green jasper spotted with red, as if with blood. Also called heliotrope.

BOGWOOD — Wood that was petrified after having been partially decayed due to its lengthy suspension in a lake, swamp or mud.

BORNITE — A brittle, metallic looking copper mineral that tarnishes easily. It sometimes gives a colorful iridescent appearance.

BOTRYOIDAL —Resembling a grape cluster in form, as the crystallization of a mineral.

BRACHIOPOD — Belonging to the phylum of marine animals with hinged upper and lower shells enclosing two arm-like parts with tentacles that are used for guiding minute food particles into the mouth.

BRECCIATED — Rock consisting of sharp-cornered bits of fragmented rock, cemented together by sand, clay or lime.

BULL'S-EYE AGATE — Agate which displays concentric circular lines resembling a bull's-eye target when cut and polished perpendicular to the banding planes.

C

CABOCHON — A gem cut style distinguished by its smooth convex top and no facets.

CALCITE — A mineral consisting of calcium carbonate crystallized in hexagonal form found in common limestone, chalk and marble.

CALCITE CLUSTERS — A cluster or group of calcite crystals.

CARLSBAD TWIN CRYSTALLIZATION — A type of crystal twinning common in feldspar, especially orthoclase. It is a penetration twin in which the twinning axis is the "c" crystallographic axis and the composition surface is irregular.

CARNELIAN — A siliceous tone and red variety of chalcedony. It is fairly hard and capable of a polish.

CARNELIAN AGATE — An orange variety of agate.

CAT'S-EYE —An effect in which a hard stone, when cut smooth, manifests on its surface and its interior, an undulating or wavy light.

CAVITY — A hole or hollow place.

CHALCEDONY — A clear and colorless agate without patterns or inclusions. A translucent or microcrystalline form of quartz that is often pale blue or gray with a nearly wax-like luster.

CHALCEDONY ROSES — An bubbly, botryoidal occurrence of chalcedony, generally found in float. The flattened and bubbly chalcedony is said to sometimes look like a flower of stone, hence the name.

CHERT — Cryptocrystalline sedimentary rock similar to flint. White, black, gray or banded chert is often found as nodules within limestone and dolomite layers.

CHROME ORE — Any rock containing substantial amounts of chromite. Such specimens are often quite colorful.

CHROMITE — A hard, black mineral that is almost infusible and insoluble when crystalline and imparts hardness to steel. It is the chief ore of chromium.

CHRYSOCOLLA — A silicate of the protoxid of copper with a fine emerald-green color, apparently produced from the decomposition of copper ores, which it usually accompanies.

CINNABAR — Red sulphic of mercury or quicksilver. It occurs in brilliant red crystals and also in amorphous masses of different shades of red and brown. It is very heavy and gives out fumes of quicksilver when heated.

CLASTIC — Consisting of fragments of older rocks.

CLINOPTILOLITE — A potassium rich zeolite mineral. A variety of heulandite.

CLUSTER — A group of crystals growing close together.

CONCHOIDAL — Producing smooth convexities or concavities like those of a clamshell when fractured associated with being brittle.

CONCRETION — Spheroidal or tuberous body of mineral aggregate formed in sedimentary rocks. A hard ball or odd-shaped mass of mineral matter. Concretions form around a nucleus such as a bone, shell, leaf or fossil.

CONGLOMERATES — A rock composed of rounded fragments of various rocks cemented together by a siliceous or other matter.

CONTACT ZONE — Aureole or a zone surrounding an igneous intrusion in which contact metamorphism of the country rock has taken place.

COPPER — A reddish-brown, malleable, ductile, metallic element that is corrosive-resistant and an excellent conductor of electricity.

CORAL — The calcareous or horny skeletal deposit produced by anthozoan or rarely hydrozoan polyps.

CRINOID STEMS — The main shaft of a crinoid which attached the flower which is attached to the sea bottom.

CRINOIDS — A family of echinoderms surviving to the present, (commonly known as "sea lily") but often found as fossils. The stem which anchored the "flower" to the sea bottom is most often recovered.

CRYSTAL — A homogeneous, solid body of a chemical element, compound or isomorphous mixture, having a regularly repeating atomic arrangement that may be outwardly expressed by natural planar surfaces called "faces."

CRYSTALLINE — Having the properties of a crystal; a regular internal arrangement in three dimensions of constituent atoms.

CUPRITE — A reddish mineral that is an ore of copper, cuprous oxide. Found massive and in isomeric crystals.

D

DATOLITE CRYSTAL — The siliceous borate of lime, a mineral of two subspecies, the common and the botryoidal.

DECOMPOSITION — Breaking up or separating into basic components or parts.

DENDRITE — A branching, treelike mark made by one mineral crystallizing in another.

DESERT VARNISH — A thin dark shiny film, composed of iron oxide with traces of manganese oxide and silica, formed on the surface of pebbles, boulders and rock outcrops in desert regions after long exposure. It is caused by exudation of mineralized solutions from within and deposition by evaporation on the surface.

DOUBLY-TERMINATED — Referring to a mineral crystal, such as quartz, which has a termination or point on one end.

DRUSY QUARTZ — Studded with small crystals.

DUMORTIERITE — Rhombic and found in some metamorphic rocks. Colors range from violet, blue to pink-violet.

DUMP — The location(s) where non-valuable discarded rock and soil are transported. Material left on the dump is regarded as too poor in quality to be of any interest to the mining process.

E

EPIDOTE — A yellowish green mineral usually occurring in grains or columnar masses, and sometimes used as a gemstone.

EROSION — The wearing away of the earth's landscape by natural forces of water, wind, ice, waves and tides.

"EYES" — Minerals or rocks which when cut in cross section, exhibit concentric, eye-like patterns usually caused by spherical inclusions.

F

FELDSPAR — Any of a group of crystalline minerals that consist of aluminum silicates with either potassium, sodium, calcium or barium and that are an essential constituent of nearly all kinds of rocks.

FIRE AGATE — A form of agate which displays an opal-like play of colors.

FISSURE — A narrow crack or opening of considerable length and depth.

FLOAT — A general term for isolated, displaced fragments of a rock, especially on a hillside below an outcropping ledge or vein.

FLOWER AGATE — Agate, which when polished, contains inclusions which look like tiny flower petals of varying bright colors.

FLUORESCE —Producing light or glowing when acted upon by radiant energy.

FLUORITE — A halide group mineral frequently purple, but also found green, yellow or blue in color.

FLUORITE CUBES — Cubic crystals of fluorite.

FLUORSPAR — Calcium fluoride, a natural formation occurring in masses and in crystalline form, varying in color, and when pure containing about equal parts of calcium and fluorin.

FORD — A shallow place in a stream or river where one can cross.

FOSSIL — Any preserved evidence of past life.

FUSILINID — Any foraminifer belonging to the suborder Fusulinina and characterized by a multi-chambered elongate calcareous microgranular test, commonly resembling the shape of a grain of rice.

G

GAD — A chisel-like or pointed bar used in mining.

GALENA — Native lead sulfide. An ore from which the lead of commerce, and often silver, are obtained.

GARNET — A group of minerals rich in calcium, magnesium, iron and manganese. A brittle and transparent to sub-transparent mineral having a vitreous luster, no cleavage, and occurs in a variety of colors. It occurs as an accessory mineral in a wide range of igneous rocks, but is most commonly found as distinctive crystals in metamorphic rocks. Used as a semiprecious stone and as an abrasive.

GASTROPODS — Any of a large class (gastropoda) of mollusks having one-piece, straight or spiral shells like snails, limpets, etc., or having no shells or greatly reduced shells, as certain slugs.

GEODE — A hollow nodule of rock usually enclosing agate and crystal formations in the center.

GRADERS — A tractor employed to level dirt roads.

GRANITE — A common igneous rock, cooled from a magma body and containing visible crystals of quartz, feldspar and mica or hornblende.

GRAPTOLITE — A small marine organism belonging to the order Graptoloidea which is characterized by a cup or tube shaped exoskeleton.

GREEN SCHIST — A schistose metamorphic rock whose green color is due to the presence of chlorite, epidote or actinolite.

GYPSUM — A soft, white mineral; hydrated calcium sulfate. Commonly formed by evaporation.

H

HARDNESS — Resistance to scratching; measured from 1 to 10 on the Mohs scale.

HEMATITE — A reddish-brown to black, rhombohedral mineral that is a major ore of iron.

Glossary

HORNBLENDE — A hard, heavy, dark-colored, monoclinic mineral that is one of the amphiboles. It is sometimes in regular distinct crystals.

I

ILMENITE — An isomorph of hematite, found as a mineral oxide of iron and titanium. Usually dark brown or black rhombohedral mineral which is an oxide of iron and titanium.

INCLUSIONS — Mineral crystals enclosed within a large host mineral specimen. Inclusions may also be gas bubbles or liquid-filled cavities.

IRON — A white, ductile and malleable chemical metal that is the commonest and most useful of all the metals.

J

JADE — Any of various ornamental green or white stones that is a silicate of calcium and magnesium. It is tough and compact, and of a resinous oily aspect when polished.

JADEITE — A translucent, usually greenish mineral found only in metamorphic rock that is a silicate of sodium and aluminum. This is the most precious type of jade.

JASP-AGATE — A combination of jasper and agate in one rock.

JASPER — An opaque cryptocrystalline quartz of any of several colors, usually red, yellow or brown.

K

KYANITE — A bluish silicate of aluminum that forms in long, thin bladed crystals that are found in high pressure metamorphic rocks.

L

LACE AGATE — Agate, which when polished, displays contrasting colors in lace-like patterns.

LIMB CAST — A mold formed when quartz filled the cavities left in dried mud by decomposed limbs and twigs. The resulting cast is often an exact replica of the original.

LIMESTONE — A sedimentary rock composed entirely or chiefly of carbonate of calcium. When containing sand or silica, it is called siliceous; containing clay, it is argillaceous; and containing carbonate of magnesium, it is dolomitic. When firm or crystalline, it is called marble.

LIMONITE — A general term for a group of brown, naturally occurring hydrous iron oxides.

LIMONITE CUBE — A cubic crystallization of the mineral limonite.

M

MAGNESITE — A light-colored, semihard magnesium carbonate mineral found uncombined, crystalline, granular or compact in form.

MALACHITE — Native carbonate of copper. Green malachite occurs in green mammillary masses, consisting of concentric layers having a fibrous structure. It admits a high polish.

MANGANESE — A grayish-white metallic chemical element, usually hard and brittle, which rusts like iron but is not magnetic. Frequently associated with iron.

MARBLE — A metamorphic rock composed of re-crystallized calcite.

MICA — Any of various colored or transparent mineral silicates crystallizing in monoclinic forms that readily separate into thin leaves.

MICROMOUNT — A small, well-crystallized specimen of a mineral that can be seen well only through a microscope.

MINERAL — A naturally occurring substance (usually inorganic) that is crystalline and has a composition that can be defined by a simple chemical formula.

MOLLUSK — A group of invertebrate animals that includes snails, clams and the nautilus.

MOONSTONE — A semitransparent to translucent feldspar that exhibits a bluish to milky-white pearly or opaline luster. An opalescent variety of orthoclase feldspar.

MOSS AGATE — A general term used in North America for any translucent chalcedony, agate, or cryptocrystalline quartz with inclusions of any color arranged in moss-like or flower-like patterns.

MOSS OPALITE — Opalite containing inclusions that look similar to moss.

MOTTLED — Marked with blotches, streaks and spots of different colors or shades.

N

NATROLITE — A hard, light-colored, orthorhombic zeolite, characterized by crystals that radiate out, often needlelike, from a central point, hydrous sodium aluminum silicate.

NAUTILOID — Any of the subclass Nautiloidea of cephalopods with chambered, coiled or straight external shells.

NODES — Central point or swelling.

NODULE — A small rounded lump of a mineral or mineral aggregate.

O

OBSIDIAN — A black or brown vitreous volcanic rock. It is similar to black glass and is primarily composed of silica.

OBSIDIANITE — Another name for an Apache tear which is an obsidian nodule that has been weathered out of a lava deposit.

OLIVINE — An hard, olive-green variety of chrysolite that is an ore of magnesium.

ONYX — Any stone exhibiting layers of two or more colors strongly contrasted, as banded jasper or chalcedony, but more the latter when it is marked with white and stratified with opaque and translucent lines.

OPAL — A mineral that is a hydrated amorphous silica that is softer and less dense than quartz. It typically has a definite and often marked iridescent play of colors.

OPALITE — A colored occurrence of common opal.

ORB — A sphere or globe.

ORBICULAR RHYOLITE — An occurrence of rhyolite containing little "eyes." Rhyolite containing a lot of spherical inclusions, which when cut in cross sections, produces surfaces filled with concentric circular patterns.

ORPIMENT — Pigment of gold arsenic trisulfide having a lemon-yellow color and a resinous luster.

ORTHOCLASE — A colorless or lightly colored mineral of the alkali feldspar group.

OUTCROP — Rock exposed at the surface.

P

PEGMATITE — A light-colored, coarse-grained, intrusive igneous rock, usually granitic that contains large crystals of quartz, feldspar, mica and sometimes rare minerals. It usually occurs in fissures and cracks of other igneous rocks.

PELECYPOD — An aquatic mollusk belonging to the class Pelecypoda. It is characterized by a bilateral symmetrical bivalve shell, a hatchet-shaped foot and sheet-like gills.

PERIDOT — A deep, yellowish-green transparent olivine.

PERLITE — A volcanic glass composed of rhyolite and containing a higher amount of water than obsidian and other more recognized forms.

PETRIFICATION — The process of fossilization whereby organic matter is converted into a stony substance by the infiltration of water containing dissolved inorganic matter (e.g. silica, calcium carbonate) which replaces the original organic materials, sometimes retaining the structure.

PETRIFIED PALM — Palm wood that has been petrified.

PETRIFIED REED — Ancient bundles of reeds that have been compacted together and petrified much in the same way as petrified wood.

PETRIFIED WOOD — Fossilized wood in which the cells of the wood have been entirely replaced by crystallized silica and thereby converted into quartz or opal.

PIT — A hole or cavity in the ground.

PLASMA AGATE — A semi-translucent green variety of chalcedony (agate) that sometimes exhibits little yellow spots.

PLUME AGATE — A variety of agate with ostrich feather-like formations.

POCKETS — A cavity filled with ore, oil, gas or water.

POCKMARK — A scar.

POROSITY — The ratio, usually expressed as a percentage, of the volume of a material's pores, as in rock, to its total volume.

PSILOMELANE — A general reference to a variety of manganese minerals frequently displaying a bubbly botryoidal occurrence.

PYRITE — A common isometric mineral that consists of iron disulfide and has a pale brass-yellow color and metallic luster. Frequently crystallized and is also massive in mammillary forms with a fibrous or stalactite structure with a crystalline surface. Also known as iron

PYRITE CUBES — Pyrite in a cubic formation.

PYROLUSITE — A tetragonal manganese dioxide mineral having a metallic luster and a dark, steel-gray color.

Q

QUARTZ — A mineral, silicon dioxide, that occurs in colorless and transparent or colored hexagonal crystals and also in crystalline masses. An important rock forming mineral.

R

RAINBOW AGATE — Agate that, when polished, exhibits the spectrum of the rainbow.

RAINBOW QUARTZ — Quartz that displays a faint opal-like play of colors.

REALGAR — A bright, orange-red, monoclinic mineral that is a combination of sulfur and arsenic in equal equivalents.

RHOMBOHEDRAL — Designating or of a crystal system having three axes of equal length, none of which intersects at right angles with another.

RHOMBS — Crystals displaying a rhombohedral structure. It is a six-sided, roughly equidimensional crystal.

RHYOLITE — A group of extensive igneous rocks. A very acid volcanic rock that is the extrusive form of granite.

ROCK — A consolidated assemblage of grains of one or more minerals.

"ROSES" — This is a shortened reference to chalcedony roses.

ROUGH — The raw gemstone.

RUTS — A groove, furrow or track made in the ground by the passage of a wheeled vehicle.

S

SAGENITE — A mineral with a needle-like spine (acicular) or crystal tetragonal form that is red oxide of titanium. The acicular crystals cross each other, giving a reticuled appearance.

SANDSTONE — A common bedded sedimentary rock composed largely of sand grains, mainly quartz, held together by silica, lime, etc.

SARDONYX — A variety of onyx made up of alternating stripes or layers of white or yellow chalcedony and sard, used as a gem, especially in cameos.

SCAR — A precipitous rocky place or cliff.

SEAM — A visible line of rock or mineral passing through a larger mass of rock, such as a seam of quartz in a limestone quarry wall.

SELENITE — A variety of sulfate of lime or gypsum occurring in transparent crystals or crystalline masses.

SEMIPRECIOUS STONES — Designating gems of lower value than those classified as precious. Examples are garnets and turquoise.

SERPENTINE — A species of stone that is usually an obscure green, mottled and unstratified and principally composed of a hydrous silicate of magnesia.

SHALE — A fissile rock that is formed by the consolidation of clay, mud or silt and has a finely stratified or laminated structure. Composed of minerals essentially unaltered since deposition.

SILICA — Silicon dioxide. A component of chert, flint, agate and quartz.

SILICIFIED WOOD — A term which includes all varieties of wood that have been converted into silica.

SILTSTONE — A rock formed from silt that has a texture and composition of shale but lacks its lamination, sometimes referred to as mudstone. It is a rock whose composition is between sandstone and shale.

SLAG — The fused refuse or dross separated from a metal in the process of smelting.

SMOKY QUARTZ — A variety of quartz occurring in shades from gray to black.

SOAPSTONE — A compact, usually impure, massive variety of talc.

SPHALERITE — A sulfide mineral found in a variety of colors, such as red, yellow, brown or black. It is often associated with pegmatites or hydrothermal minerals, such as galena and chalcopyrite.

STRATA — A single layer of sedimentary rock.

STRINGERS — Thin mineral veins or filaments, usually occurring in nonparallel patterns within a host rock or mineral.

SULFUR — A pale-yellow nonmetallic chemical element found in crystalline or amorphous form.

T

TAILINGS — Waste or refuge piles left from various processes of milling, mining, distilling, etc.

TALC — A soft, light-colored, monoclinic mineral with a greasy feel that is a magnesium silicate.

THOMSONITE — A mineral of the zeolite family, occurring generally in masses of a radiated structure with a glassy or vitreous luster. It is a hydrous silicate of aluminum, calcium and sodium.

TRAPEZOIDAL CRYSTALS — Crystals that have two parallel sides.

TRAVERTINE — A finely crystalline, massive deposit of calcium carbonate that is white, tan or cream color. It is formed by checmical precipitation from solution in surface and ground waters, as around the mouth of springs, especially hot springs. It also occurs in lime caves, where it forms stalactites and stalagmites. A spongy or less compact variety is tufa.

TRILOBITE — Extinct Paleozoic marine arthropods having the segments of the body divided by furrows on the dorsal surface into three lobes.

TUFF — A porous igneous rock, usually stratified, formed by the consolidation of volcanic ash, dust, etc.

TUMBLER — A revolving box or drum into which loose materials are loaded and tumbled about as for mixing, polishing, etc.

TUMBLING — The act of using a revolving box or drum into which loose materials are loaded and tumbled about for use in mixing or polishing.

TURQUOISE — A greenish-blue, hard mineral that is a hydrous copper aluminum phosphate.

TURRITELLA AGATE — Agate containing silicified gastropod shells.

U

UVAROVITE — An emerald green garnet with small crystals and is a calcium chromium silicate.

V

VARIEGATED — Marked with different colors in spots, streaks; partly-colored.

VARIETY — A named specific color or other quality of a gemstone species, such as ruby for red corundum.

VEIN — A continuous body of minerals, igneous or sedimentary rock, etc. occupying a fissure of zone, differing in nature from the enclosing rock.

VOLCANIC GLASS — Natural glass, as obsidian, formed by the very rapid cooling of molten lava.

VOLCANIC TUFF — A porous igneous rock, usually stratified, formed by the consolidation of volcanic ash, dust, etc.

VOLCANISM — The process of extruding magma, lava or ash to the earth's surface.

VUG — A cavity or hollow in a rock or lode, often lined with crystals.

W

WASH — Eroded soil that has been transported by running water. The broad, gravelly, normally dry streambed, often located at the bottom of a canyon.

WEATHERED — Stained, worn or beaten by the weather.

WHISK BROOM — A small, short-handled broom for brushing clothes, etc.

WONDERSTONE — A banded rhyolite.

WOOD AGATE — Agatized wood in which the structure of wood is plainly shown.

X

Y

Z

ZARATITE — An emerald-green mineral often found with chromite, in or as a crust on various igneous rocks.

ZOISITE — A hard, glassy and orthorhombic mineral that is often regarded as a variety of epidote. It is a hydrous calcium aluminum silicate and occurs in deeply striated rhomboid prisms, much compressed and rounded. Its colors are gray, yellowish- or bluish-gray, brown, grayish-yellow or reddish-white.

NOTES

OTHER TITLES AVAILABLE

*Available at your local rock shop,
outdoor store or retail bookstore.*